THE OPEN UNIVERSITY

Arts: A Third Level Course
A361 SHAKESPEARE

BLOCK VI

King Lear

Prepared for the Course Team by Graham Martin

The Open University Press

The Open University Press
Walton Hall, Milton Keynes
MK7 6AA

First published 1984. Reprinted 1987

Designed by the Graphic Design Group of the Open University

Printed in Great Britain by
Adlard & Son Ltd
The Garden City Press
Letchworth, Herts.

ISBN 0 335 11215 3

This text forms part of an Open University course. The complete list of units in the course appears on the back cover of this text.

For general availability of supporting material referred to in this text, please write to Open University Educational Enterprises Limited, 12 Cofferidge Close, Stony Stratford, Milton Keynes, MK11 1BY, Great Britain.

Further information on Open University courses may be obtained from the Admissions Office, The Open University, PO Box 48, Walton Hall, Milton Keynes, MK7 6AB.

1.2

Contents

Study Material

The Study Material for Block VI consists of the following:

THE CORRESPONDENCE TEXTS

TELEVISION

Programme 8	King Lear Workshop 1
Programme 9	King Lear Workshop 2

PERFORMANCE CASSETTE

Cassette 5(p)

Side B	Lear

RADIO

Justice and Power in *King Lear* by Professor Frank Kermode

The set text for this block is the New Penguin edition of *King Lear*, edited by G. K. Hunter.*

Acknowledgements

I would like to thank my colleagues on the course team, and Professor Molly Mahood, the course assessor, for helpful advice and comments on the drafts of this block.

GM

*Hunter, G. K. (ed.) (1972) *King Lear*, Penguin New Shakespeare edn.; hereafter referred to as the *set text*.

Introduction

WE have allotted three units to help you with your reading of *King Lear*, the second of the two plays (the first being *Antony and Cleopatra*) which we expect you to know more fully than the other texts in the course. *King Lear* is also a very substantial text which requires—and generously repays—much reading and thinking about. Clearly, your first step must be to read the play *at least once* before spending any time on these units. There is no reason why this should not be a quick reading, where you don't pause much over particular puzzles about the meaning of speeches, the sometimes obscure sequence of events, or larger problems of interpretation, though of course you will begin to have first thoughts about these. You should then read the play a second time, consulting the notes to the text whenever necessary. When you have completed this second reading, you should spend a couple of hours making your own notes on any features of the play that have impressed you, and particularly about the issues listed at the end of this introduction. A discussion of these provides most of the material for Part One of this block. Its aim is to make you reasonably familiar with the text, so that you can then embark on Part Two which discusses some main interpretations of the play as a whole. The point there is to invite you to engage on your own terms with critical debates about *King Lear*, and to re-read particular scenes and passages in the light of such debates. Part Three opens up the more general question of tragedy, with reference to *King Lear*, but also to other Shakespearean examples of the genre.

The set text, edited by G. K. Hunter, is equipped with explanatory notes which you should regularly consult, once you have completed your first reading. There is also an excellent introduction, probably best read in connection with Part Two of this block, where I will be referring to it.

Issues to concentrate on, once you have completed your two readings of *King Lear*, are:

(1) Why does Cordelia give her father so abrupt and unyielding an answer to his question in I.1.82–6?

(2) Why are there two distinct 'stories'—Lear's and Gloucester's?

(3) Why does the Fool have such a prominent role in the early acts?

(4) Why is Lear's 'madness' so central to the play?

(5) What do you make of the play's overt harshness (as instanced in the blinding of Gloucester, and the death of Cordelia)? Do such events make it 'pessimistic'?

Remember that this seemingly simple question 'why?' must be explored in terms of the whole play, leading you from one speech or scene to another, and yet another, and back again, to and fro and round and round, until you develop an overall grasp of the play's various details and structure.

NOW READ THE PLAY

Part One
Preliminary Issues

Cordelia's abrupt and unyielding answers in I.1.82–96

IT will be useful first to summarize the main events of Act I. There are five scenes, introducing us to all the participants of the play, and sketching the relationships between them that are responsible for what follows.

Act I scene 1

Gloucester and Kent briefly discuss the news of the King's plan to abdicate. Edmund is introduced to Kent as Gloucester's illegitimate son. Lear announces to his court that he intends to abdicate, dividing the kingdom between his three daughters. Gonerill and Regan respond eloquently to his request for an expression of love and gratitude, but Cordelia refuses to comply. In a rage, Lear revokes his first plan, divides the kingdom into two, half each to the elder daughters, both of whom are married, and he disinherits Cordelia. The King of France, one of her two suitors, agrees to marry her without the expected dowry. Meanwhile, Kent, Lear's experienced and faithful counsellor, criticizes Lear's action in respect of Cordelia, and is himself banished for his pains. The scene closes with a brief, private discussion between Gonerill and Regan showing them in a different light from their previous public behaviour.

Act I scene 2

In a soliloquy, Edmund reveals his unscrupulous and ambitious nature. Although the illegitimate son, he determines to replace his brother Edgar, as heir to Gloucester's lands and title. Gloucester appears, worrying about the abdication scene he has just witnessed. Edmund lets him see a supposed letter from Edgar inviting Edmund to conspire against Gloucester's life. Gloucester, taken in by this, instructs him to investigate more fully and bring Edgar to him to explain himself. Gloucester leaves. Edgar appears, and Edmund tells him to keep away from his father who is furiously angry with him. Edmund concludes that with 'a credulous father and a brother noble' (l. 175) his scheme will soon succeed.

Act I scene 3

We move from Lear's court to Gonerill's castle. A brief exchange follows between Gonerill and her steward Oswald, about the behaviour of Lear, his Fool, and his knights now that they reside *chez* Gonerill. Gonerill instructs Oswald not to attend Lear's demands; she wants to bring the situation to a head.

Act I scene 4

Kent turns up, disguised as Caius, determined to serve Lear. Lear angrily responds to the negligent behaviour of Oswald. The Fool indirectly gibes at Lear for giving up his power. Gonerill appears and complains to her father about the behaviour of his Fool and his retinue. Lear responds in a fury: he denounces Gonerill's ingratitude and savagely curses her. He decides to leave at once and reside instead with Regan. Albany (Gonerill's husband) ineffectively tries to calm matters. Gonerill instructs Oswald to carry a letter to Regan, warning of her father's impending arrival.

Act I scene 5

Lear sends the disguised Kent ahead with letters for Regan, forewarning of his arrival and the reasons for it. There are further gibes from the Fool. Lear fears that the situation may drive him mad. Lear, the Fool, and some of the knights begin their journey to Regan's castle.

Here are three possible explanations of Cordelia's behaviour which might have occurred to you.

(1) All plots require an initial act of disruption to create the forward-moving momentum necessary to engage our interest. In the Lear plot, this stems from Cordelia's refusal to say what is expected of her. Shakespeare simply chooses to begin the story in this way, and no further explanation is required.

(2) Cordelia is a chip off the old block, stubborn, with a touch of her father's self-righteousness. Shakespeare wants to underline this family trait as the seed of the whole painful story.

(3) Shakespeare wants to set up a contrast between public and political relationships, and private personal relationships. Lear's request to the daughters confuses this key distinction. Cordelia's refusal to play his game points to the moral superiority of the second ('so young, my lord, and *true*' (l. 108)).

You will see that these are different sorts of explanation, relating respectively to *plot*, *character*, and *theme*, so none necessarily excludes another. See what evidence you can find for them.

---

(1) A general statement about plots ('all plots require . . .') cannot be defended on the basis of only one, but if you glance back over the other plays you have read in the course, you will see that it works quite well.

1 *Henry IV* The King's plan to go to the Holy Land is checked by news of Glendower's rebellion, more seriously by his disappointment that his son doesn't behave like a prince, a point immediately brought out by Hal's first scene with Falstaff.

Twelfth Night The Duke's scheme to woo Olivia receives a check; and the shipwrecked Viola resolves to start her new life in Illyria disguised as a young man.

Hamlet The appearance of the Ghost to Hamlet disrupts the political state of affairs set up by the accession of Claudius and his marriage to Gertrude.

If this kind of analysis interests you, follow it through for the other set plays. Or does it seem too formalist, a mere exercise in making abstract comparisons? It is, at any rate, one way to bring home the fact that plays involve the construction of stories. Any story must have a beginning which then *leads somewhere*, otherwise why should we stay to listen, or watch, or read? To sketch in a general state of affairs, and then disturb it, is an excellent way to set up this forward-pressing narrative movement.

What is the state of affairs disrupted by Cordelia's blunt 'nothing'? There is the 'darker purpose' (l. 36) announced by Lear in his first speech—his decision to divide the kingdom into three parts to be ruled by his daughters and sons-in-law, a political event ('the division of the kingdom', l.4) which is the first thing the audience hears about in the opening exchange between Gloucester and Kent. Cordelia's refusal to answer her father in the manner of Gonerill and Regan radically checks the unfolding of his scheme, and sets going the chain of events which is the play. And the point of underlining this is to set a limit to our curiosity about Cordelia's behaviour. This initial situation is Shakespeare's *donnée*, his 'given' narrative premise. It is as if he is saying: 'Suppose, for a moment, the following situation. The favoured third daughter of this particular king decides not to go through with a public display of "love" on the occasion of his abdication. I know it sounds a bit fantastic, but just suppose it possible, what might then happen?' The way Shakespeare sets up this story shows that he doesn't want us to worry overmuch about the whys and wherefores of the opening, but rather to listen to, and to watch, what follows.

The Love Test in I.1. A scene from Kozintsev's film King Lear *(1972). (Courtesy of National Film Archive/Stills Library)*

Is it a *stable* state of affairs that Cordelia disrupts? Hardly. What Cordelia checks is Lear's intentions for the future, rather than a previous condition. Is it only in Lear's mind that these plans have an existence? Or did other people know about them? Well, we do have that opening exchange between Kent and Gloucester which makes it clear that Lear's general plan was no secret. So in that sense, Cordelia's refusal to play the Lear game challenges an initial set of assumptions. But we don't know whether the Court knew about Lear's plan for a public exchange of political power for declarations of love by his daughters. How do you take the phrase '*darker* purpose'? The set text editor glosses this as 'hitherto undivulged' which does suggest that Lear is springing a surprise on the Court. But is he also springing a surprise on his three daughters? If you were producing the play, would you suggest that he is—so that their speeches are, as it were, extempore? Or would you make it clear that they had been forewarned about the business, knew what their father expected of them, so that the whole thing becomes a public charade played by the Lear family (in the secret) for the benefit of the Court (who are to be surprised)? That is a possibility surely? We could then say that the state of affairs Cordelia disrupts is a family ritual (Lear demanding love from his daughters) all too familiar to the daughters.

One other possibility should be canvassed: that Cordelia's refusal to speak brings into question Lear's wisdom in dividing his kingdom in the first place so that *that* decision, taken at some earlier point, becomes the truly disruptive event. Why should this be considered? Did you have thoughts about Lear's abdication plan? Kent responds to Lear's rejection of Cordelia by advising him to 'reserve thy state' (l. 149), that is 'hold on to your power'. Gloucester in the next scene expresses alarmed amazement (I.2.24) at what happened, while in later scenes the Fool gibes at Lear for giving up his personal power. No one, though, seems to express any major political objections. Indeed, Regan thinks her father took too long to make up his mind (II.4.245).

Yet here, as Elizabethan scholars remind us, we need to exercise our historical imagination. Think back to the *Henry IV* plays. We can see clearly, I think, that Elizabethan worry about the smooth succession from one royal authority to the next is explicitly addressed in those plays. The stability of the Elizabethan state had depended, so it seemed to contemporaries, on the life of its monarch, and then on the uncontested succession of James VI of Scotland. Consider the impact of the opening scene of *King Lear* against such a history: a strong ageing monarch proposing to divide his kingdom amongst three sets of rulers, one of whom is the

King of France! How could this not strike a contemporary audience as a recipe for political disaster—civil war, or foreign invasion, or both? And if we remember the play's later events—rumours that Albany and Cornwall are manœuvring against each other, that the King of France is about to invade the kingdom, and does eventually send an army—we can see that Shakespeare kept this political dimension in place, a frame within which the fates of the characters are played out. In sum, from a political angle, there was a stable state of affairs which *Lear himself has disrupted*. Why? We do not know. Old age, he says. But why abdicate in this most politically dangerous of ways? We do not know. Here, we come up against another element in the play's *donnée* ('just suppose . . .' says Shakespeare), one guaranteed to engage the real political hopes and fears of those Jacobean audiences, for whom James I had only recently come to power, after a period of intense political anxiety about what *might* happen when Elizabeth I died.

(2) I suggested that the three different explanations of Cordelia's answer didn't rule each other out, but you may now conclude that if it is, in the end, Shakespeare's way of getting the play going, the question of her actual motives disappears. Still, what did you decide about the notion, adopted by several producers of the play, that Cordelia has a self-righteous streak that must attract some blame for what follows? How would you direct the actress playing the part? Should we see here an aspect of that obdurate and steely will which Lear boasts of (his behaviour in the storm scenes bears him out), and which both Gonerill and Regan display in their treatment of their father? To put the point differently, does Shakespeare offer producers some latitude of interpretation about Cordelia's behaviour, or does he make it clear what attitudes and feelings govern her behaviour and speech in this scene?

Read the scene over again if you haven't clarified your ideas.

My own view is that Shakespeare has been quite remarkably explicit about the sources of Cordelia's behaviour. Had her *first* words been 'Nothing . . . nothing . . . I love your majesty/According to my bond, no more nor less' (I.1.87–93), it would have been open to a producer to 'read in' as sub-text, a kind of legalistic and self-approving temper, a stubborn Lear-like *personal* determination to obstruct her father's emotional claims. But in fact, Cordelia's first speeches are 'asides' to the audience, by means of that non-realistic convention Shakespeare uses so often (Prince Hal, Hamlet, Edmund, etc.) to explain what a character is up to. Cordelia has two such 'asides', following her sisters' speeches of declared love:

> What shall Cordelia speak? Love, and be silent.
>
> (l. 62)

> Then poor Cordelia!
> And yet not so, since I am sure my love's
> More ponderous than my tongue.
>
> (ll. 76–8)

We might still want to cling to the chip-off-the-old-block explanation at the level of settled will-power. The pressures on Cordelia to shift her ground are evident enough and her resistance is impressive. But the notion of self-approving virtue could only be supported by interpreting these 'asides' as, in a profounder way than Gonerill's and Regan's, hypocritical. We would have to conclude that Cordelia was entirely self-deceived about loving her father better, more genuinely, than her sisters. But do subsequent events support that? Surely not. Remember Cordelia's actions in Acts IV and V. I think these 'asides' are Shakespeare's way of preparing us for Cordelia's behaviour as 'given', to stop us probing into motives.

'Sir, I love you more than word can wield the matter': Gonerill, I.1.55. A scene from Peter Brook's film King Lear *(1971). (Courtesy of National Film Archive/Stills Library)*

He invited us to 'suppose' such a person as Cordelia, and leaves it at that.

And indeed, if we stand back a little from this particular episode, is it not also true that in the comparison with characters like Antony, Cleopatra, Macbeth, Lady Macbeth, Othello, Hamlet, the characters in *King Lear* are delineated simply and straightforwardly, in effect, without explanation? *Why* are Gonerill and Regan so hard and cruel? We don't know. *Why* is Kent loyal to the point of self-destruction? No answer (except that of the Fool that Kent *is* 'a fool'). Why is Gloucester so easily persuaded that Edgar is a villain, and why doesn't Edgar make a point of seeing his father so as to clear things up? Again, no real answer. *King Lear* is a play in which, against Shakespeare's common practice, the characters are not probed for their deeper and more elusive motivations and impulses. It is not a play of 'psychological realism', the kind of play which makes it easy to mistake Shakespeare for a nineteenth-century novelist. Which is not, of course, to imply that it doesn't have something to say about human reality. To be sure, characterization of this kind makes difficulties for modern productions—this is a direct consequence of such a view. Actors, producers, audiences—we are all accustomed to expecting answers to the question 'Why does so-and-so behave in that way? What complex undertow of relationships accounts for this surface action?', and if we don't get them we are apt to retort that the dramatist hasn't conceived his characters in sufficient depth and consistency, and in thinking like this we touch upon an extensive cultural and moral assumption of our times. So, is *King Lear* a play in which we have to meet a challenge to this assumption? In the case of Cordelia, might not the actress playing the first scene have to say, 'I can give no clues as to Cordelia's motives here. She is a good character; her sisters are not. It is as simple—and difficult—as that'. What do you think?

(3) What evidence did you find for the view that Shakespeare wants to set up a contrast between public and political relationships, over and against personal and private relationships? Cordelia seems to illustrate the second, her sisters the first; Burgundy, with his calm worldliness, the first (no dowry, no marriage), and France the second (Cordelia is a dowry in herself). And then there is Kent, the honest counsellor who stands up for personal truth ('Be Kent unmannerly/When Lear is mad', ll. 145–6), against the prudential counsels of *realpolitik*, and suffers the consequences. So there seems to be a pattern here.

Did you notice anything about the way the characters speak which might support this? Have another look at the scene. How would you describe the style of speech of Lear, Gonerill, Regan, as against that of Cordelia and Kent?

Would you agree that the first three make *speeches*, a performance the other two either refuse, or take on with reluctance? Cordelia implicitly protests against the *kind* of speaking demanded of her.

> *Lear* Nothing will come of nothing. Speak again.
> *Cordelia* Unhappy that I am, I *cannot* heave
> My heart into my mouth . . .
>
> (I.1. 90–2)

What she has to say cannot be uttered in speeches. Kent, on the other hand, though he adopts a plain manner, makes rather a powerful speech of his own. Experienced in court affairs, he commands a public idiom well enough to debate effectively with the King, who is reduced to the speechlessness of personal violence to shut him up (ll. 139–66). But Kent shares with Cordelia a deep distaste for what we might call 'courtly speech', where words bear no relation to intended deeds, where the speaker (Lear, Gonerill, Regan) disjoins language and feeling, so that the first disguises one set of feelings by claiming to articulate a quite different set, or where the speaker uses language to fence and parry with the listener, hiding his/her true meanings behind it. (Contrast Regan and Gonerill's *prose* exchange which closes the scene, with their flowery public speeches.)

Yet there is a problem about seeing this as opposition between public *falsity* and private *truth*. The two realms of discourse are set in contrast, yet the fact that Kent can speak in both underlines a significant complication. This opening scene about 'the division of the kingdom' is pre-eminently a public affair. We may reasonably speculate about earlier behind-doors political negotiations between Lear, Albany, Cornwall, France and Burgundy (he actually refers to some about Cordelia's proposed dowry), where the real decisions were made. Following this line, critics and producers often represent the public ceremony of Lear's abdicatory speeches as a routine formality, not unlike today's Queen's Speech at the opening of a new Parliament, personally delivered by her but written by the Prime Minister as a reflection of the plans of the Government. But such an approach is tainted by a modern anachronism. Lear's public kingly existence is not a shell, a decorative uniform for some inner private reality to which, after his abdication, he can securely retreat. Having surrendered royal power, and finding his personal authority contested, how does he respond? As to a radical challenge to his personal *identity:* 'Who is it that can tell me who I am?' And the Fool replies: 'Lear's shadow' (I.4.226–7). When he denounces Kent, it is in the courtly style. When he curses Gonerill and Regan, again the speech is elaborate, formal, constructed.

Yet there is no question here of smoothed-tongued eloquence aiming to deceive. Lear's ferocious comminations on those who oppose his will cannot be thought to lack *sincerity*. He means every word of them. Then again, if we glance back at Cordelia's 'rejection' speech it includes these words:

> . . . I love your majesty
> According to my bond, no more nor less.
>
> (I.1. 92–3)

And she goes on to explain what this 'bond' is: a set of duties which she owes Lear, as king and father. Cordelia, that is, defends her refusal to say more than 'nothing' on the grounds of these feudal public relationships: Lear has been a good father and king, and she a good daughter and subject. Moreover (here perhaps we note a touch of Lear's argumentative spirit), she adds that if she married, she would owe half her love to her husband, so that her sisters are in error in offering all their love to Lear. Kent's personal bluntness, too, is justified in terms of 'duty' (l. 147). It is the public duty of a good counsellor to warn his ruler, at whatever personal risk, against a rash or unwise decision. We might even think of the whole scene in implicitly allegorical terms: the King, seduced by Flattery (Gonerill, Regan) against the virtue and advice of Good Counsel (Kent, Cordelia).

Yet, of course, we also sense a more complex handling of the crisis than that. Evidently, Cordelia is the favourite daughter, with whom, as he says, the ageing Lear expected to spend his remaining years (ll.123–4). Indeed, it is Lear who introduces the 'personal' note into the public declarations of gratitude and love. Faced with Cordelia's reasonable point about loving according to her bond, Lear barks back: 'But goes thy *heart* with this?' (l. 105). Evidently, he is demanding more than formal recognition, public tributes. And the savage character of his rejection (see ll. 108–20) of Cordelia, however couched in the terms of legitimate responsibility ('paternal care,/Propinquity and property of blood'), bespeaks feelings of a different order and source than the 'courtly' public debate can account for. If you happened to see Peter Brook's film of *King Lear*, you will recall that Paul Schofield portrayed the King in the opening scene as a suspicious and gloomy paranoid, muttering his requests and replies, conveying an extraordinary sense of barely-controlled murderous anger. This, in its turn, may be thought to simplify, turning Lear into a psychological 'case'. But that some such feelings and impulses are at work in the abdication scene is surely difficult to deny.

Lear and the Fool leave Gonerill's castle, I.5. (Brook's King Lear.) *(Courtesy of National Film Archive/Stills Library)*

What I would like to suggest is that Shakespeare is presenting us with a contrast, not so much between deceitful public protestation and private candour, as an insight into *the category of the political*, where relationships however *apparently* personal (as within a royal family they must seem) are really governed by political considerations. We hear Gonerill and Regan making their loving avowals at one point; only a few minutes later, they are speculating on the *political* threat inherent in Lear's decision to reside with them, bringing with him the considerable force of 'a hundred knights' (l. 133). They do not think of Lear as an ageing father who requires care and attention, but as a continuing danger to their political authority. And with reason. When Lear storms out of Gonerill's castle, what does he say?

> . . . Thou shalt find
> That I'll resume the shape which thou dost think
> I have cast off for ever.
>
> (I.4.305–7)

Lear intrudes into this political state of affairs a quality of 'personal' feeling that has no proper place in it. And while it is clear that Cordelia and Kent are morally preferable to Gonerill and Regan, in the sense of being trustworthy and undeceiving, what this illustrates is that the 'political' has no place for the 'moral': the issues, the language, the relationships are entirely different, perhaps irreconcilable. Those who speak up for the 'moral' are forced into silence (Cordelia) and banishment (Kent). Lear uses a language of morality, but it is a false use. He is entirely preoccupied with power, and (the most striking example of that slender knowledge of himself which Regan mentions (l. 292–3)) has no understanding that, far from wanting to be rid of power, he passionately wants to hang on to it. Can we not suggest that it is from this knot of inner contradiction that his rages, both impressive and ludicrous, actually flow?

We have spent some time on this opening scene, but not, I hope you will agree, a disproportionate amount. It initiates the main story to a degree rare in a Shakespeare play. It is a kind of narrative 'explosion', whose dreadful results we then, painfully, have to follow to their end. Let us now look more briefly at the other questions I began by raising on page 5.

Lear and retinue leave Gonerill's castle, I.5. (Brook's King Lear.) *(Courtesy of National Film Archive/Stills Library)*

Are there two distinct 'stories'?

Why are there two distinct 'stories'—Lear's and Gloucester's? It will be useful first to review the main events of Act II.

Act II scene 1

We have moved from Gonerill's castle, the place for the last three scenes of the previous act, to the home or castle of Gloucester. Edmund appears, and receives news that Regan and her husband will arrive there the same night, wherein he sees an opportunity to advance his fortunes. Edgar appears, Edmund tells him he is in danger, pretends Gloucester is coming, stages a mock fight, then urges Edgar to fly. He then calls in Gloucester, accuses Edgar of having invited him to join in a scheme to murder their father, whereupon he fought him and Edgar escaped. Gloucester sends his servants to capture Edgar, tells Edmund he is a 'loyal and natural boy' (l. 83). Regan and Cornwall arrive, and hear the story. They praise Edmund, and then explain to Gloucester their reason for coming: the news of Lear's differences with Gonerill.

Act II scene 2

Kent, bearing Lear's letters for Regan, meets Oswald, bearing Gonerill's letters for Regan, at Gloucester's home. (We may suppose that both have been re-directed from Regan's castle, where they were sent in the previous act.) Kent picks a quarrel, recognizing Oswald as the servant of Gonerill who had offended Lear. Edmund, Cornwall, Regan and Gloucester appear, and Cornwall demands an explanation, as a result of which, Kent is put in the stocks, despite Gloucester's appeal that as the King's messenger, he should not be so treated. Kent, stocked, soliloquizes on the changeableness of Fortune, and reveals that he has had a letter from Cordelia.

Act II scene 3

This is a soliloquy from Edgar, explaining that in order to avoid capture he will disguise himself as a half-naked 'Bedlam beggar' (l. 14), changing his identity from 'Edgar' to that of 'Poor Tom' (ll. 20–1).

Act II scene 4

Lear arrives at Gloucester's castle, finds Kent in the stocks, and reacts angrily, while the Fool gibes intermittently. Gloucester appears, and Lear demands to see Regan and Cornwall. Shortly, they appear, and Lear speaks of Gonerill's behaviour, appealing to Regan to treat him as he deserves. Lear then raises the question of *why* Kent was put in the stocks. Whereupon Gonerill arrives, and Lear discovers that the sisters make common cause against his claims. He turns from one to the other as each cuts down the number of knights they will accept. Regan's conclusive 'What need one?' (l. 258) prompts a final denunciatory speech from Lear, and with his few supporters, he leaves Regan's castle. Gloucester appeals on Lear's behalf, but Gonerill, Regan and Cornwall insist that Lear be left to his own devices, and instruct Gloucester to close up the gates.

Let me now suggest some possible answers to the 'two stories' question.

(1) The Lear 'story' in itself didn't employ all the available talent in Shakespeare's company (the King's Men), so the Gloucester 'story' provided useful extra parts.

(2) The Lear 'story' was in itself too thin, and Shakespeare's audiences were accustomed to the variety of theatrical interest provided by double plots.

(3) Shakespeare wanted to generalize some of the issues raised by Lear's experience, which would otherwise have rested on too slight a fictional basis.

(4) Shakespeare wanted to introduce a different, but complementary set of issues, by means of the Gloucester 'story'.

Will you now make your own notes in response to these suggestions, before reading further.

(1) and (2) You may have thought these two possible reasons for the introduction of the Gloucester 'story' trivial, a matter of externalities. But are they? We know almost nothing at all about Shakespeare's creative practice. Did he, like a novelist such as Graham Greene, settle down every morning to his daily task of slogging out three hundred lines of blank verse? Did he sketch out his plots before writing the speeches? Did he provide his actor colleagues with a rough draft, which they tried out in rehearsal, Shakespeare then modifying what he had written in response to their criticisms? (As a playwright Samuel Beckett habitually works closely with producer and actors. 'Poetic' dramatists like T. S. Eliot and W. B. Yeats successively changed their drafts as a result of rehearsals.) We can only guess, though on the basis of contemporary comments on Shakespeare's fluency and speed in composition, it seems reasonable to suppose that he wrote his plays in bursts, rather than by painstaking and steady effort. Nevertheless, a process of close collaboration with his fellow-actors of the King's Men seems highly probable. We should not think of Shakespeare as a brooding genius turning out his plays in lonely seclusion. Rather, he worked in a sort of actors' and writers' co-operative, a group who owned their own theatre, theatrical properties, acting scripts; and a key to whose remarkable record of artistic and financial success over nearly thirty years lay in this shared and sustained commitment to their joint venture. (The general programmes on Cassette 1 include some information on this point.) It is therefore reasonable to suppose that Shakespeare would need to take into account the number of actors' parts which any new play he was working on would make available. By introducing the Gloucester 'story', three excellent parts would be added (Gloucester, Edmund and Edgar) and a small one (the Old Man in IV.1), and in the case of Edgar, a demanding and varied role. Of course, this can only *be* a speculation, but it's worth floating, if only to remind us that Shakespeare's plays were the product of a particular theatrical situation, as well as a product of their author's mind.

The second suggestion, that the audiences expected the variety of incident made possible by double plots, has positive evidence in its favour. Double plots are a very common feature of Elizabethan and Jacobean plays, and audience expectation may very properly be considered as one factor in the way Shakespeare planned his plays. Yet we would want to add that, in the case of *King Lear*, while Edgar's role as Poor Tom adds an unexpected dimension to Lear's experience, the Gloucester 'story' as a whole doesn't exactly provide *variety* of incident, so much as a further proliferation of macabre and terrible scenes. (By contrast, in the *Henry IV* plays, the Falstaff sub-plots provide an entirely different *kind* of scene from those deriving from the main political plot, comedy in prose against plottings and battles in lofty blank verse.) In *King Lear*, we can see that Shakespeare adapted the double-plot convention or practice to his aims for the whole play. Moreover, compared with the sources from which Shakespeare took the Lear 'story', his version *is* less varied in interest. Of the several relationships and characters that might have been developed, Lear alone receives full characterization, and his tale (contrast the variety in *Antony and Cleopatra*) reduces to one single strand: the results of I.1. So this could have been a reason for introducing the additional story of Gloucester and his sons.

(3) and (4) What did you think about these two possibilities? Granted that we notice elements shared by both stories, as well as some that are not, how explicit has Shakespeare made the connections and how seriously does he intend them? Can you point to scenes or speeches which act as clues to the audience that we should see the stories in relation to each other? If none springs to mind, look again at your text before going any further: in Acts I, III and IV.

Gloucester surely draws an obvious parallel between his and Lear's situation in his superstitious speech to Edmund:

> These late eclipses in the sun and moon portend no good to us . . . This villain of mine [i.e. Edgar] comes under the prediction: there's son against father; the King falls from bias of nature: there's father against child . . . and the noble and true-hearted Kent banished!'
>
> (I.2.103–16)

But Gloucester at this point doesn't see the significance of the comparison. For him it's just a sign of bad times. So the speech is clearly intended as a clue to the audience to notice connections. But then, in III.4, with the entry of Edgar disguised as Poor Tom, the parallel between Lear, expelled into the storm by his hard-hearted daughters as much against the 'bias of nature' as Lear's treatment of Cordelia, and Edgar, expelled from family and society by Edmund's false accusation and his father's credulity, becomes very close, articulating thereby a central theme of the play. It is Tom's behaviour that finally pushes Lear into madness, and who then comes to symbolize, in Lear's mind, the essential condition of humanity: 'Unaccommodated man is no more but such a poor, bare, forked animal as thou art' (III.4.103–4). Here, then, the two stories weld tightly together. Shakespeare clearly wants us to think about their interconnection as a key to what, as a whole, the play is about. And a third example of an unmistakably explicit connection appears in IV.6, when the mad Lear meets the blinded Gloucester, an exchange to which we must return.

Bearing these points in mind, we can now see more clearly that, though Lear's story dominates throughout, the Gloucester story is interwoven with it, from the play's first moments when Gloucester and Edmund appear before the abdication scene. We can see, too, why Shakespeare brings all the principals together in II.2 at Gloucester's castle, so that both sisters, and Cornwall as well, are implicated in Lear's rejection; and why in the next scene, we learn of Edgar's plight, which places him in the vicinity of Lear's wanderings in the storm. By the time we reach Act III, the alternations between the 'mad' outdoor scenes involving Lear, the Fool, Poor Tom and Kent, and the events in Gloucester's castle that lead to his being blinded begin to resemble a set of variations on a broadly similar theme.

In what ways do you think the two stories raise *different* (even if complementary) issues? I would suggest at least two contrasts. First, neither Gloucester nor Edgar seem to deserve their fates, as we surely feel Lear does. 'Deserve' perhaps puts the point too strongly; I mean only that Lear is in large measure responsible for what happens to him. His 'story' unfolds straightforwardly from the two major blunders he makes in I.1: the division of the kingdom, and the banishment of Cordelia. In the most literal sense Lear chooses his fate: rather than make an accommodation with his daughters, he walks out into the storm, which is also an internal, mental storm. Lear is not a victim, not at all 'More sinned against than sinning' (III.2.60), and his heroic stature derives directly from that fact. Gloucester, by contrast, may bear *some* responsibility for events, but is more of a victim of forces beyond his control. Of course, Edgar does say to his dying brother that 'The dark and vicious place where thee he [i.e. Gloucester] got/Cost him his eyes' (V.3.170–1)? True enough as *cause* (Edmund's bastardy was the motive behind the treachery which put Gloucester in Cornwall's power). Yet the punishment seems disproportionate, to say the least, putting aside the fact that it is actually Gloucester's loyalty to Lear that prompts Albany's vicious treatment. Then, Edgar's fate is surely the direct responsibility of Edmund, not of any foolish or wicked act of his own. Or are we to assume that his trust in his brother was so stupid as to merit severe penalty?

The other main difference between the Gloucester and Lear 'stories' is raised by Gloucester's suicide attempt. This brings in issues not directly touched in Lear's experience.

What do you think Shakespeare is saying by means of Gloucester's 'suicide'? We'll come back to it later, but meanwhile you might like to consider the scenes between Edgar (variously disguised) and his father from IV.1 till V.2, Gloucester's final appearance on stage. The suicide attempt belongs within this sequence.

Before leaving this question of the two 'stories', a word about Shakespeare's sources for *King Lear* may be helpful. The Lear story had been popular since the Middle Ages, appearing in many different versions, from which we can deduce that it would be known to Shakespeare's audience. There had also been a previous stage version, *The True Chronicle History of King Leir*, belonging to the 1590s, but republished and perhaps acted again in 1605. Shakespeare's more important source was the second edition of *The Chronicles of England, Scotlande, and Irelande* (1587) by Raphael Holinshed, a book you will have heard about already in connection with the sources of the *Henry IV* plays. Shakespeare also took details from other contemporary accounts, but in none of these sources for the Lear story was there any basis for the story of Gloucester, Edgar and Edmund. Here Shakespeare drew upon another source altogether, Sir Philip Sidney's romantic narrative *Arcadia* (1590). You will find both the Holinshed and Sidney sources printed in the Appendix. You might like to read them now, as a change from discussing *King Lear* itself, and note any major alterations Shakespeare has made. Meanwhile, one point is very clear: a playwright who makes use of two such different sources, and adapts them in such a way that they fit together in the same play, is evidently working to a deliberate plan. You may recall from Cassette Programme 3, the talk by Professor Molly Mahood about Shakespeare's reading, and her emphasis on its creative and constructive spirit. The relation of *King Lear* to its principal sources is a further striking demonstration of her argument.

The Fool's prominent role in Acts I–III

Why does the Fool have such a prominent role in the early acts? Here are some comments for you to consider.

(1) In III.1, a conversation between Kent and a Gentleman, tells us that Lear, having left Gloucester's castle, is now wandering about in the storm, his only companion 'the Fool, who labours to out-jest/His heart-struck injuries' (ll. 16–17). Is this the Fool's principal function: to distract Lear from obsession with his daughter's ingratitude?

(2) George Orwell, contesting Tolstoy's view that the Fool was 'a tedious nuisance', proposed that

> his jokes, riddles and scraps of rhyme, and his endless digs at Lear's high-minded folly, ranging from mere derision to a sort of melancholy poetry . . . are like a trickle of sanity running through the play, a reminder that somewhere or other in spite of the injustices, cruelties, intrigues, deceptions and misunderstandings that are being enacted here, life is going on much as usual.*

Do you agree?

(3) In Block III *Twelfth Night*, Cicely Havely writes about the place of Fools in Renaissance and aristocratic houses. How far does Shakespeare's presentation of the Fool in *King Lear* draw upon this real social background?

*Orwell, G. (1966) *Collected Essays*, Heinemann, p. 423.

Before reading further, look back over scenes which include the Fool especially in Acts I and III, and see how far the text supports/confutes such arguments.

---

(1) Shakespeare often uses minor characters, or as here, an otherwise anonymous character, to say important things. (You will find another case in IV.3, where an anonymous Gentleman (perhaps the same one) informs Kent about Cordelia's reaction to the news of Lear's ill-treatment.) So what the Gentleman says about the Fool must be taken seriously. It reminds us that Shakespeare didn't suppose his more complex scenes had a self-evident meaning, and that by such hints and directions, he wanted his audience to attend to them in a particular way, to engage in an active process of 'interpretation'. III.2 broadly supports what the Gentleman has said. It opens with a long speech by Lear invoking the elements in support of of his feelings about Gonerill and Regan, interspersed with remarks and a song from the Fool attempting to mitigate Lear's rage. You will find other such cases in III.4. Yet is that the only effect? Following the first part of Lear's speech ('Blow, winds, and crack your cheeks! Rage! Blow!' III.2.1), the Fool says:

> O nuncle, court holy-water in a dry house is better than this rain-water out o'door. Good nuncle, in; ask thy daughters' blessing. Here's a night pities neither wise men nor fools.
>
> (III.2.10–13)

But Lear pays no attention, and continues with his invocation ('Rumble thy bellyful! Spit, fire! Spout, rain!' (l. 14). The Fool's next intervention is a song, whose first three lines (ll. 27–9) your editor glosses as:

> the man who finds a home for his penis before he has a roof over his head is destined for lice-infested beggary.
>
> (*Set text*, p. 244)

Jokey enough in its sardonic style, but is the song intended to distract Lear? Is Lear *listening?* In a moment, Kent enters and addresses him, but Lear is utterly absorbed in his inner debate, calling on the gods to seek out the wicked, imagining himself both as a sort of judicial investigator of hypocrites, and as 'a man/More sinned against than sinning' (ll. 58–9). Only at the end of this speech does he show any sign that he knows the Fool is there (ll. 68–9), while to Kent he gives no spoken recognition. So while the Fool may be *trying* to distract Lear from 'his heart-struck injuries', he certainly isn't succeeding, and if we look again at his actual words, don't they have clear implications for the *audience?* What does his first remark mean? Have you consulted your editor's gloss on 'court holy-water'? (Do so now if you haven't; see page 244 of the set text.)

Broadly, we can interpret the Fool's remark as 'better to flatter the powerful [i.e. Regan and Gonerill] and do what they ask, than stay out in the storm'; and with 'here's a night pities neither wise men nor fools' he implies that however eloquently and impressively Lear rages against the elements they will pay him no attention whatsoever. His comments, that is, offer the audience a different perspective on Lear's situation: realistic, unillusioned, commonsensical.

And what of the song? Certainly, down-to-earth, sensible, a piece of popular wisdom (don't raise a family if you have no house or money), but also of only indirect application to Lear's situation; that is, Lear has been the opposite of realistic, hence his present position. The Fool's two further contributions to this scene are also songs, one delivered *after* Lear has left the stage. Must we not then conclude that the Fool has a most important role *vis-à-vis the audience*, as well as his role *vis-à-vis* Lear?

If you now glance back over the Fool's contribution to earlier scenes, you will find this borne out. See, for example, I.4 and II.4, and ask yourself what, as audience, we learn about Lear's situation from the Fool's jokes, witticisms and snatches of song.

(2) Orwell thinks that the Fool provides an implicit commentary on the action as a whole, and not just temporary relief for Lear. What did you think of this? We have seen that his comments in III.2 express a down-to-earth realism which brings an ironic perspective to bear on Lear's behaviour. In your review of earlier scenes, did you find this effect? I would be surprised if you hadn't. In I.4, the whole burden of the Fool's jokes is that Lear simply hasn't grasped the truth of his situation. To quote just one of many examples, when Gonerill enters, and Lear asks why she looks so cross, the Fool cuts in with:

> Thou wast a pretty fellow when thou hadst no need to care for her frowning. Now that art an 0 without a figure. I am better than thou art now; I am a fool; thou art nothing.
>
> (I.4.187–90)

Or again, when Gonerill makes her speech about the riotous behaviour of Lear's followers (ll. 196–209), and Lear responds with his partly sarcastic, partly bewildered 'Who is it that can tell me who I am?' (l. 226), the Fool tells him: 'Lear's shadow' (l. 227). A third case, from II.4, is the Fool's exchange with Kent, sitting in the stocks:

> *Kent* How chance the King comes with so small a number?
> *Fool* And hadst been set i'the stocks for that question,
> thou'dst well deserved it.
>
> (II.4.61–3)

Kent, that is, should have foreseen that Lear, having yielded power to his daughters, would soon find his train of knights being cut down. Noticeable, too, in such scenes is the fact that many of the Fool's remarks are directed as much at the audience, as at Lear himself, who often gives vague or no replies. And to underline for the audience that what the Fool says *is* important, Shakespeare has Kent (disguised as Caius) remark after one of the Fool's quips about Lear having given his power away, 'This is not altogether fool, my lord' (I.4.149).

So, Orwell is surely right in conceiving the Fool's role as that of commentator on the play's action, certainly in so far as it involves Lear. But do you agree that his general effect is to remind us that despite the intrigue and the cruelty enacted in play 'life is going on much as usual'? We can see what Orwell is getting at, but my own view is that the Fool's comments add up to a more precise and less comforting message—that politically Lear's action was a disaster. And might there not be an element of malice in many of the Fool's remarks? As the King retorts after one crack about the link between lands and rent and power, 'A bitter fool!' (I.4.134). The Fool's situation is, after all, precarious. Lear is his only protector. Lear's mistakes have direct and painful consequences for the Fool, as well as for Lear. He is also in Lear's power: Lear more than once threatens him with a whipping. Being the dependant of so irascible and self-absorbed a person as Lear must have meant hourly uncertainty about how one might be treated. Some, at least, of the Fool's 'bitter' jokes can reasonably be seen as a way of getting his own back for the plight which Lear's folly has brought about. We should, that is, beware of sentimentalizing the Fool.

(3) Lear's Fool is, as you will have seen from Cicely Havely's account of Feste in *Twelfth Night*, quite close to the real Fools who were a feature of Renaissance courts. He is 'all-licensed' (I.4.196), privileged like Henry VIII's Fool Will Somers, to joke at the expense of the powerful. (Doubtless, that is why Gonerill particularly dislikes him: we can suppose that she has heard some of his remarks to Lear about the results of his abdication.) He is intelligent, bawdy, knows

popular sayings and songs, plays with words, and enjoys doing so. (Indeed, this is a trait of all Shakespeare's Fools.) And as I suggest above, while he has a certain privilege and freedom, he is finally dependent on the King's favour, as a real Fool would be. One further point, though may be added. You will perhaps recall from my contribution to Block V *Measure for Measure* (pp. 61–5), the traditional staging practice which Shakespeare exploits in his handling of Pompey. The Fool in *King Lear* is similarly identified with a sensibility and voice that we must call 'popular', and which the differential staging practice of the Elizabethan productions provides with a particular theatrical *locus*: down-stage, in direct relation to the audience. As we have seen, we derive from the Fool's comments an ironic perspective on Lear's situation. His remarks are as much for the audience, as for on-stage consumption. So while Shakespeare drew upon real social conditions, he also used his material in a new way, adapting theatrical practice to the expression of a more complex view of Lear's situation than could be derived from any other character in the play. Kent can tell Lear that he is rash, but he is then banished. Only the Fool can tell him that he has become a 'shadow' (I.4.227), and get away with it.

Lear's madness

Why is Lear's madness central to the play? Here is an initial exercise which should help to clarify the issues.

> Check through the text noting the points when madness first threatens Lear, when it overcomes him, whether it goes through distinct stages, and when he recovers. *Don't read any further till you have done this.* Then, consider the following comments.

---

(1) Other texts in this course will have shown that Shakespeare seems to be interested in 'madness' (Malvolio, Ophelia, Hamlet), and more generally in the phenomenon of extreme mental disturbance (Lady Macbeth, Othello, Timon, Leontes). Lear's 'madness' is then at the centre of *King Lear* because it gives Shakespeare the chance to explore the condition of mental breakdown at length and in detail.

(2) Lear's 'madness' is no more than a theatrical device by whose means Shakespeare expresses his own critical political opinions in oblique form.

(3) Dr Johnson explained the blinding of Gloucester on the ground that 'our authour well knew what would please the audience for which he wrote'.* Lear's 'madness' was similarly directed towards the satisfaction of a Jacobean taste for the macabre and grotesque (for which other playwrights of the day provide much evidence).

My 'chronology' for Lear's state of mind is:

(i) After his quarrel with Gonerill, and just before setting out for Gloucester's house, where he expects to find Regan, Lear is partly mulling over what has happened, partly attending to the gibes of the Fool. He then says:

> O let me not be mad, not mad, sweet heaven!
> Keep me in temper; I would not be mad!
>
> (I.V.43–4)

Temper, here, means not our modern 'good temper' but 'balance', 'under control', as in our modern 'temperate'.

*Raleigh, Walter (ed.) (1908) *Johnson on Shakespeare*, Oxford, p. 161.

(ii) At Gloucester's house, faced with Regan's cold reception, madness begins to threaten Lear, though he doesn't at first call it that. When he asks Gloucester for a second time to announce him to Regan and Cornwall, he mutters more or less to himself:

> O me, my heart, my rising heart! But down!
>
> (II.4.116)

The next provocation is Regan's suggestion that he should return to Gonerill:

> I prithee, daughter, do not make me mad.
>
> (II.4.214)

Then following the discussion about how many followers Lear *really* needs (concluded in Regan's final thrust 'What need *one?*'), Lear bursts out with 'O, reason not the need!', denounces both sisters, pleads to the gods for patience, and then prophesies (II.4.259–81):

> O Fool, I shall go mad!

These words are preceded by the stage direction 'storm and tempest'.

(iii) In the storm scene, Kent finds Lear raging at the elements and suggests he come out of the wind and rain into the hovel. Lear replies: 'My wits begin to turn'. But he then speaks to the Fool in an unexpectedly thoughtful way, certainly not 'mad':

> Come on, my boy. How dost my boy? Art cold?
> I am cold myself. Where is this straw, my fellow?
> The art of our necessities is strange
> And can make vile things precious. Come, your hovel.
> Poor fool and knave, I have one part in my heart
> That's sorry yet for thee.
>
> (III. 2.67–73)

(iv) Two scenes on, Lear is still being persuaded by Kent to enter the hovel, is still brooding angrily on his daughters' behaviour, and says:

> Your old kind father, whose frank heart gave all!
> O, that way madness lies; let me shun that;
> No more of that!
>
> (III.4.20–2)

(v) Lear's madness begins later in this scene when, disturbed by the Fool's entry into the hovel, Edgar emerges 'disguised as Poor Tom', utters scraps of nonsense, to which Lear responds with:

> Didst though give all to thy daughters? And art thou come to this?
>
> (III.4.47–8)

Of course, this might be a sarcasm, in the vein of Lear's satirical denunciations, and so it could be played. Indeed, some lines later Kent says no more than 'His wits *begin* t'unsettle' (l. 155). But by this point Lear is calling Poor Tom a 'philosopher' (l. 147) and 'learnèd Theban' (l. 150), genuinely supposing he is a wise man. If by 'madness', we mean such delusion, then clearly at this stage Lear *is* mad. (The satirical point, in other words, is being made by Shakespeare: Tom is wise in having plumbed the corruptions of social life and seen them as they are.)

(vi) Two scenes later, now inside the hovel, we are presented with the 'mad' trial when Lear, as judge, supported by Edgar and the Fool, tries Gonerill and Regan for their crimes. Kent at the end of this scene says that had Lear been able there and then to sleep soundly, instead of being taken at Gloucester's urgent request to Dover, he might have recovered his senses (III.6.95–8).

(vii) Cordelia gives an account of Lear 'mad as the vexed sea', wandering about in the fields near Dover; she sends out soldiers to find him (IV.4.1–8); and discusses with the Doctor how he might be cured.

(viii) Following Gloucester's attempted suicide, Lear meets him and Edgar, 'fantastically dressed with wild flowers' (IV.6.79), still in the grip of the delusions of the trial scene. Yet, in his exchange with Gloucester, Lear talks very intelligently (see, for example, the speech about 'the great image of authority' (IV.6.158–73), which Edgar calls 'reason in madness', and evidently recognizes Gloucester (l. 178). Here, then, is a mixture of delusion and sanity.

(ix) Rescued by Cordelia's soldiers, Lear is given rest and sleep, and on waking is evidently in his right mind once again (IV.7.45 ff.).

(x) In the play's final scene, Lear may be again on the verge of madness. When he appears bearing the dead Cordelia in his arms, he seems very uncertain of Kent's identity (V.3.280–7). But the better explanation is surely that he can attend to nothing but Cordelia's death.

Lear's state of mind is thus a prominent aspect of four of the play's acts; the Lear 'story' is, for all practical purposes, the story of his loss and recovery of sanity. I would distinguish five stages. The first is Lear's fear of going mad, marked by furious denunciations of Gonerill and Regan, and a notable self-absorption. He sees himself as a pure victim of his daughers' ingratitude, having in no way contributed to the catastrophe. The second stage, still infused with revengeful anger against his daughters, broaches more general themes. We hear not just of the injustice *he* suffered, but of injustice as such; not only of *his* sufferings in the storm, but of the Fool's, and of the outcast generally (the 'poor naked wretches' he speaks about in III.4.28 ff.). The third is the condition of complete delusion, the trial scene, and the fourth is the scene with Gloucester, where Lear is calmer, with glimpses of sanity, though still in the main deluded. The fifth is his recovered state after the reconciliation with Cordelia.

Let us now look at Lear's condition in the light of the comments on p. 20.

(1) Hamlet's madness is partly put on, his 'antic disposition' a tactical mask to distract the Court's attention while he investigates Claudius's responsibility for the death of his father. Yet also, we learn from Ophelia that Hamlet *is* in a bad way, and his behaviour occasionally suggests someone on the verge of insanity. Here, Shakespeare surely reveals a concern with the sources of mental breakdown. Hamlet is shown to us as nearly overborne by a complex of painful feelings and ideas arising from two sources: (a) directly personal wounds inflicted by Claudius, Gertrude and, unwittingly, Ophelia, and (b) a sense of 'ideological' distance from the ideals and practices expected of somebody in his position in that particular political and social milieu. Yet Hamlet does not, in Lear's sense, suffer a thorough-going breakdown. So, to revert to the notion I proposed about Cordelia's situation at the beginning of the play, we might think of Shakespeare as saying to us: 'let us just *suppose* that a man like Lear decides to give up his royal authority in this way, a man moreover who had "ever but slenderly known himself" (I.1.292–3), how might the situation develop?' Like Hamlet, Lear suffers direct wounds from his family; but unlike Hamlet, he has inflicted some on himself, and, 'ideologically' speaking, he is not in conflict with Gonerill and Regan. His quarrel with them is about power, and who shall wield it, not about 'ideology'. So, in one sense, Lear does reflect Shakespeare's analytic preoccupation with 'madness', taken a stage further than Hamlet's case, and developed more *single-mindedly*. We never think of Lear pretending to be mad; we see the actual process of disintegration; its

immediate causes are vividly present to us.

Would you want to go further? Is the play constructed primarily so that Lear's state of mind can be thoroughly explored? Is that the reason why most of the other characters and possible narrative developments are foreshortened and simplified?

In practical stage terms, it does seem clear that the space allotted to Lear's mental state ruled out more than sketchy treatment of other possibilities. Act III, for example, intercuts the storm scenes with the narrative development of the Gloucester plot, the developing liaison between Edmund and Regan, the news about Cordelia's army, received both by Gloucester and Kent, all handled in brief laconic scenes which follow upon each other with bewildering speed. In Act IV, the exchange between Lear and Gloucester, and the scene of Lear's recovery dominate a bustle of other briefly sketched events: Cordelia's arrival, Albany's denunciation of Gonerill, Oswald's toing-and-froing between Regan and Gonerill, Kent's puzzling behaviour, Edgar's discovery of Gonerill's letter to Edmund encouraging him to kill Albany, signs of the approaching battle. Then, if we look at the content of Lear's delusions, we find a constant factor: the wish to revenge himself upon Gonerill and Regan. His denunciatory speeches in Acts I and II culminate in the rhetoric of impotence:

. . . No, you unnatural hags,
I will have such revenges on you both
That all the world shall—I will do such things—
What they are yet I know not; but they shall be
The terrors of the earth . . .

(II.4.273–7)

Denied real power to 'punish home' (III.4.16), Lear takes refuge in delusory states where he can take imaginary revenge on the 'pelican daughters' (III.4.72) The trial scene itself is a mere cover for his desire to cause them pain ('To have a thousand with red burning spits/Come hissing in upon 'em!' III.6.15–16). In the scene with Gloucester, after the speech about 'the image of authority' revealing that Lear has learned something important about those who sit in judgement on others, he is still lusting for revenge:

It were a delicate stratagem to shoe
A troop of horse with felt. I'll put't in proof;
And when I have stolen upon these son-in-laws,
Then kill, kill, kill, kill, kill, kill!

(IV.6.185–8)

And, in the recovery scene, when the Doctor tells Cordelia that 'the great rage . . . is killed in him' (IV.7.78–9), we notice that instead of wanting to punish others, Lear now sees himself as the proper object of punishment. His first words to Cordelia are:

Thou art a soul in bliss; but I am bound
Upon a wheel of fire, that mine own tears
Do scald like molten lead.

(IV.7.46–8)

The inner coherence of these changes in Lear's state of mind is strong evidence that Shakespeare had developed a distinct view of 'madness'. Lear's characterization is in a different mould, in this respect, from Hamlet's. Lear's 'madness' becomes, in fact, his route to sanity, if by that we mean a better understanding of the self and its relations with others. Looking back on the Lear of I.1, from the vantage point of Act IV, we might even suggest the Lear begins the play in so unbalanced a state of mind as itself to deserve the term 'mad', and that the subsequent process of his 'madness' is a coming-to-terms with his own overbearing, emotionally greedy, and self-dramatizing personality.

So, in summary, I think that both the detailed exploration of Lear's state of mind, and the severe curtailment imposed upon other possibilities in the story, together suggest that Shakespeare did build the play round the issue of Lear's 'madness'.

(2) But let us now look at a different possibility. Did you find any evidence for the notion that Lear's 'madness' provided Shakespeare with a vehicle for the expression of politically subversive thoughts and feelings?

It should be said immediately that this is a tricky line of approach. The history of Shakespearean criticism is strewn with the bleached remains of hypotheses of this kind. Deducing what Shakespeare may or may not have thought *in propria persona* is entirely dependent on 'evidence' drawn from the plays, and since he was inconsiderate enough to leave no separate account of his beliefs, religious, political, social or moral, we have no external guide as to which plays embodied his personal conclusions about the issues of his time. To take a case in point, the critic E. M. W. Tillyard argued persuasively for the existence of an 'Elizabethan World Picture', an article of Shakespearean belief substantially and sympathetically rendered in the cycle of Shakespeare's History plays, characterized by a stable social and political hierarchy headed by a divinely-appointed monarch. But granted that such views are uttered by certain characters in many plays, there is not only no certainty that *Shakespeare* 'believed in' them, but evidence that he might *not* have comes all too readily to hand. How else are we to understand his fascination with what another critic, John F. Danby, has called the theme of 'killing the King'?* Order certainly, yet an order repeatedly disrupted and its legitimacy challenged—isn't that a truer representation of the *Henry IV* plays (even of *Hamlet*) than the idea that they implicitly underwrite a general conception of hierarchic stability? And we must always keep in mind that Shakespeare's plays are not discursive essays in political and social theory, but *fictions*, in which certain human possibilities are, so to speak, *tried out* in imaginary form. That is the underlying reason why you should be sceptical about any discussion of Shakespeare's plays which tries to allot their author a fixed set of beliefs about the world.

But given these general caveats, what of *King Lear*? Is it entirely fantastic to suppose that Lear's character offered Shakespeare the chance to air some ideas, by no means easily to be construed as support for the status quo? Consider, for a moment, the fact that *King Lear* was performed at the Court of James I of England on 26 December, 1606. How do you think James might have reacted to this latest production by the acting company that bore his name (bearing in mind the fact that he held more than usually emphatic views about the divine source of kingly authority)? We can reasonably imagine him shaking his head at Lear's proposal to divide the kingdom, sharing Gloucester's alarm over the abdication, responding favourably to Lear's appeals to the gods to back him up, and seeing the Fool's jokes against Lear's folly in surrendering power as clear political good sense. Indeed, as we go through the play it is clear that Shakespeare is careful to present Lear, even *in extremis*, as an impressive figure. During the storm scenes Kent always addresses him very respectfully: Gloucester at clear personal risk early takes Lear's side (III.3.12); and after Lear has set off for Dover, Edgar's rounding-off speech concludes with 'What will hap more tonight, safe 'scape the King!' (III.6.112). Despite his abdication, all the good characters go on calling Lear 'King', and even at his most zany, in the meeting with Gloucester near Dover, his kingliness is insisted on. The blind Gloucester falls to his knees when he hears Lear's voice, asking 'Is't not the King?', to which Lear, 'fantastically dressed

*See Danby, John F. (1948) *Shakespeare's Doctrine of Nature: A Study of King Lear*, Faber, pp. 141–67.

with wild flowers' though he may be, replies 'Ay, every inch a king' (IV.6.107), and when Cordelia's soldiers find him, and Lear thinks he's been captured, we find this:

> *Lear* Come, come, I am a king; masters, know you that?
> *Gentleman* You are a royal one, and we obey you.
>
> (IV.6.200–1)

These references have a more complex effect, according to their context, than that of mere obeisance to royalty. But Shakespeare does seem to have gone out of his way to ensure that nobody could accuse him of presenting in the figure of Lear disrespectful slights at the expense of royalty or kingship. In so far as Lear's tribulations are his own fault, the lesson is that a King with his wits about him would not act as Lear does in I.1; in so far as they are caused by others, they amount to a clear denunciation of self-seeking and hard-hearted subjects, who deserve (and in the end come to) a variety of sticky ends. All of this we can presume would have met with the approval of James I.

But is that the whole story? Glance back over the Lear scenes in Acts III and IV. Do you notice any speeches in which Lear expresses ideas which, closely considered, might have given James I pause?

We have touched briefly on one such topic already: Lear's unexpected concern for the Fool; that first explicit gesture of recognition that others may suffer as well as himself (contrast his reaction to the sight of Kent in the stocks: Lear takes it only as an insult to his dignity). And this humane impulse precedes the powerful speech beginning 'Poor naked wretches, whereso'er you are,/That bide the pelting of this pitiless storm' (III.4.28 ff.), where we suddenly get a glimpse, as if from a lightning-flash, of a world outside Lear's court in which his present physical state, shelterless, cold, hungry, soaked to the skin, is an everyday occurrence. The key sentence in this speech is, surely, the self-critical 'O, I have ta'en/Too little care of this!', and lest we miss the logic of this fellow-feeling for the 'wretched of the earth', the speech ends in a diatribe against the greed of the rich and powerful, amongst whom almost all the characters in the play have to be numbered. And perhaps also that Court audience of the play on 26 December 1606?

The second topic is surely Lear's later denunciation of legal authority, as, for example, in the speech which Edgar calls 'reason in madness', a nudge to the audience that Shakespeare does not want Lear's speeches all written off as nonsensical raving.

> Thorough tattered clothes great vices do appear;
> Robes and furred gowns hide all. Plate sins with gold,
> And the strong lance of justice hurtless breaks;
> Arm it in rags, a pygmy's straw does pierce it.
>
> (IV.6.165–8)

The idea that the legal institutions and practices of society, as a system of punitive enforcement, work merely against the poor has—must we not agree—remarkable implications?

We have no way of knowing how such speeches affected contemporary audiences. But so much of what Lear says in his 'madness' turns on the psychological sources and operations of political and legal authority, that we must suppose the theme to have been deliberate on Shakespeare's part. The 'mad' Lear becomes the voice of distinctly critical views about the world formulated in speeches of notable cogency and penetration. In other words, while Shakespeare does seem to have conceived Lear as a study in mental breakdown, he so handles the development as to make room for something other than a merely 'personal' dimension. The psychological analysis is accompanied at several points by social and political analysis—or if that puts the case too strongly, let us say by social and political *questioning*, evidently planned and sustained.

As course team colleagues have pointed out, in debating the contemporary reverberations of such ideas in *King Lear*, and what Shakespeare might have been up to in making the mad king their mouthpiece, we must nevertheless beware of easy conclusions. Swift remarks in one of his writings that 'satire is a sort of glass [i.e. mirror], wherein beholders do generally discover everybody's face but their own'.* To James and his court, to its other contemporary audiences, the play told a story about the distant *past*. Moreover, plays that evidently had immediate application to the times were soon dealt with. The mere actors of a performance of *Richard II* (where a king is forced to abdicate) arranged by the supporters of the Earl of Essex in his abortive rebellion against Queen Elizabeth, were interrogated by the authorities for their possible complicity. Ben Jonson, George Chapman and John Marston, authors of a play called *Eastward Ho!* (1605) which included a satirical allusion to Scottish courtiers prospering under James I's rule, were jailed for their offence. So, *King Lear* must certainly not be thought a play '*about* the Jacobean court'. There was, too, an old tradition, strongly represented in medieval poetry of moral criticism of the corruption of the legal process by the rich and the privileged, and of their cruel indifference to the poor. As you will remember from *Hamlet* and *Measure for Measure* Shakespeare had already provided such critical sentiments with a sympathetic theatrical presentation. Their occurrence in *King Lear* clearly isn't a sudden upswelling of subversive thinking on Shakespeare's part. What we may legitimately point to is the unprecedented depth and penetration of his handling of the matter. Chekhov, pressed for his solutions to the social problems reflected in his plays, replied that the artist's business was not to produce solutions but to ask questions. In *King Lear*, we may surely think of Shakespeare asking questions about legality, privilege, power, poverty, cruelty, both personal and institutionalized, in just such a Chekhovian spirit.

(3) What is the bearing of these arguments on the third suggestion?

Look back at it again (p. 20), and reconsider your initial thoughts.

Did you begin by dismissing the idea as inappropriate to Shakespeare? Does it go against the grain to suppose that a playwright of his stature, at the height of his powers, would bother to accommodate the fluctuations of popular taste? Or even, would you agree with the view that Shakespeare most unhappily allowed popular taste to influence his plays, *much to their detriment*? The poet Robert Bridges, for example, thought that 'veneration for [Shakespeare's] genius' involved the risk of 'degrading ourselves to the level of his audience, and learning contamination from those wretched beings who can never be forgiven their share in preventing the greatest poet and dramatist of the world from being the best artist'.† This puts the point with unusual animus, but the basic argument is not uncommon. And the problem with it—putting aside the issue of whether Shakespeare's audience *deserves* such criticism—is that it assumes a Romantic view of the writer/artist/playwright as working on his own, without regard to the audience who will read or view his work. The point has already come up in our discussion of the double-plot aspect of *King Lear*, where we saw that Shakespeare adapts this familiar structure of Jacobean plays to his own purposes, making the Gloucester–Edmund–Edgar situation a complement and an extension of the themes raised in the main plot. So here, with this question of a popular taste for macabre and grotesque scenes

*Swift, J. (1919) *Gulliver's Travels*, etc., Oxford, p. 540.
†Bridges, Robert (1926) *The Influence of the Audience on Shakespeare's Drama*, Oxford, p. 29.

which 'madness' easily makes available. Just consider for a moment the 'mad' scenes in the play: Lear tears off his clothes, hails a near-naked, crazy beggar as 'the thing itself! Unaccommodated *man*' (III.4.103), then greets him as supremely wise, and a 'most learned justicer' (III.6.21); Edgar as Poor Tom suffers terrifying hallucinations, 'possession' by evil spirits; in the trial scene, a mad King, Edgar acting as mad, and a professional Fool, conduct a trial of imaginary criminals, the action punctuated by a mixture of madman's gibberish, sardonic jokes, and genuine delusion; and in Act IV, as we have seen, the mad Lear appears, bizarrely dressed, conducts a riddling exchange with Gloucester, and then runs off the stage as if in some children's game of catch-can, shouting 'Sa, sa, sa, sa' (IV.6.203)—ample material, surely, to satisfy popular taste?

But here, of course, we have to remember points (1) and (2). If Lear's 'madness' reflects psychologically consistent thinking on Shakespeare's part, as well as providing an opportunity to dramatize some trenchant criticisms of his society, then it's clear that Shakespeare has successfully adapted aspects of popular taste to his own purposes. The implication to be resisted is that Shakespeare merely followed popular taste. The relationship was an interchange, a taking-up by Shakespeare, of established and well-liked aspects of contemporary drama, and then a reworking of them on his own terms.

The play's harshness and 'pessimism'

What do you make of the play's harshness? Is the overall effect 'pessimistic'? Here are some quotations drawn from the play:

(1) *Gloucester* ... But I shall see
The wingèd Vengeance overtake such children.
Cornwall See't shalt thou never. Fellows, hold the chair.
Upon these eyes of thine I'll set my foot ...
Regan One side will mock another. Th'other too!

(III.7.64–70)

(2) *Gloucester* As flies to wanton boys are we to the gods;
They kill us for their sport.

(IV.1.36–7)

(3) *Albany* ... If that the heavens do not their visible spirits
Send quickly down to tame these vile offences,
It will come—
Humanity must perforce prey on itself
Like monsters of the deep.

(IV.2.46–50)

(4) *Edgar* The gods are just, and of our pleasant vices
Make instruments to plague us.

(V.3.168–9)

(5) *Albany* The gods defend her [i.e. Cordelia] Bear him hence awhile.
Edmund is borne off
Enter Lear with Cordelia in his arms, followed by Second Officer and others
Lear ... She's gone for ever.
I know when one is dead and when one lives;
She's dead as earth ...

(V.3.254–9)

Which of these seem to you best to represent the *overall* effect of *King Lear?* Don't proceed until you've made your choice. I will say nothing myself about these quotations since they bring up questions about the play as a whole, the subject of Part Two of this block.

GM

Regan and the blinded Gloucester, III.7. (Brook's King Lear.) *(Courtesy of National Film Archive/Stills Library)*

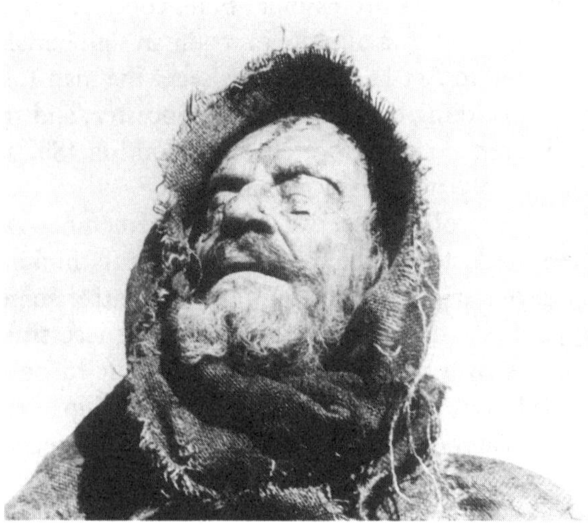

'When shall I come to the top of that same hill': Gloucester in IV.6. (Brook's King Lear.) *(Courtesy of National Film Archive/Stills Library)*

Forum

Lear, Nature and the parental bond

. . . the bond cracked 'twixt son and father. (I.2.108–9)

What do we really feel about Lear? Not *King Lear* the play, which no doubt moves to pity at the succession of harrowing experiences suffered by the aged king, but Lear the man. Is it not a common reaction to find that he provokes a certain irritation and impatience? Do we not share with Kent and the Fool, and even with Gonerill and Regan, some measure of exasperation at his 'hideous rashness' (I.1.151), the lack of fundamental discernment that prompts his sanguine, overweening and self-interested generosity? At the foreseeable disaster of his abdication from power in the expectation of a compensatory gratitude? At his hyperbolic transports of rage in his consequent disillusion? At his want of sense and moderation generally?

With *Hamlet*, the case is quite different. We appreciate Hamlet for his lively, mobile intelligence, his quick perceptions, his wit, his irony, his imagination. He carries us with him. He is engaging because he *understands* the significance of men and events, even when he knows that he is helpless to control them. He knows a hawk from a handsaw. He sees into the characters around him with an intuitive and piercing clarity that could not be further from Lear's ponderous obtuseness, his pitiful, groping search for enlightenment. Hamlet goes to his fate like Pascal's 'thinking reed', in a state of awareness. 'The readiness is all' (V.2.216). But Lear, almost until the end of the play, is painfully without insight into himself or others, particularly those who are nearest and *therefore* (as he supposes) dearest to him. Contrast his initial treatment of Kent and Cordelia with that of Gonerill and Regan (and correctly diagnosed by them at I.1.288 ff.).

Each inevitable link in the chain of rebuffs unleashed by his original act of folly comes to him as a fresh surprise, excites him to new outpourings of emotion. He must undergo the most cataclysmic torments, including madness, before he can begin to 'see reason'. He must learn like a child, or rather he must unlearn much that he took for granted as king.

The question remains: do we find Lear an attractive and sympathetic character? My guess is not always, but that we feel that we should. We have mixed feelings. What, I suggest, makes us uncomfortable and ambivalent about Lear is his fatherhood. Paternity is the compelling link that joins him to his audience. As sons and daughters ourselves, we are bound up to some extent in his relationship with *his* daughters. We trust that we are not as fearfully vindictive, not as 'unnatural', as Gonerill and Regan; but surely we share *something* of their impatience at the antics, uncontrolled, self-dramatizing, self-pitying and sometimes ridiculous, of the old man? Our reserve, however, is tempered, as theirs is not, by a sense of shame. Lear is a challenge to our accepted notions about the filial bond. Bonds can be oppressive. And Gonerill, Regan and Edmund treat the very idea of the bond as mere pious convention, without real sense or validity. They strike out, brazenly and callously, at the bond, and with a shocking directness which in Edmund's case at least is far from unintelligent. Like those other villainous outsiders, Iago and Richard III, Edmund is positively exhilarating as the hero of amoralism, a dynamic embodiment of the triumph of the will. He mocks the familial bond with outrageous realism. Why respect a parent at all, he implies, if he is indeed what the Fool calls Lear: a fool? The play provides a tension to which we react uneasily. A moral absolute—'Honour thy father'—clashes with the fierce promptings of animal self-interest. Why is the latter, as Edmund asks, less 'natural' than the former?

The answer, if any, seems to be in terms of a categorical moral injunction that draws no line between 'deserving' and 'undeserving' parents. Cordelia and Edgar obey it, regardless of the harm done to them by their foolish old fathers. Each honours his parent 'according to my bond'. By the same reasoning, Hamlet is bound to avenge his father and not to take revenge against his mother. The bond appears to be a pillar of Shakespeare's moral order, and its overthrow, as in *King Lear*, presages general collapse. The bond between parent and child is the most basic and elemental. It is anterior to the bond between siblings or spouses. In *Hamlet* Claudius broods on the 'primal eldest curse' (III.3.37) which a brother's murder involves. Gonerill and Regan have not of course murdered their father, but their extraordinary (and unexplained) cruelty towards him is presented as something akin to patricide, and certainly contrary to Nature. 'Let them anatomize Regan, see what breeds about her heart', says Lear. 'Is there any cause in nature that makes these hard hearts?' (III.6.75–7). Gonerill, Regan and Edmund ignore or mock such inhibitions as irrational taboos. Lear's parental curse is dismissed as ravings.

Yet a clear distinction is drawn between their 'nature' and Lear's. Regan and Gonerill are repeatedly and notoriously compared to monsters. Their 'natural law' is the law of the jungle, the right of the stronger, more ruthless or more wily. They respect only superior force or cunning. Like beasts and birds of prey to which they are constantly likened (kite, serpent, wolf, vulture, boar, cur, adder), and like Caliban in *The Tempest*, they do possess reason, but of a kind that is entirely self-willed and self-regarding, directed solely to the gratification of selfish purposes and animal desires. Gonerill and Regan fight like she-cats over Edmund. Morally they *are* monsters, untouched and unredeemed by 'natural' human feeling. No scruples of pity, remorse, or even self-respect stand between them and the objects of their zeal—'Tigers, not daughters' (IV.2.40).

At the same time, by the operation of another kind of 'natural law', their very liberation from 'the bond' is their undoing. Rejecting 'natural law', they themselves become rejects of nature—inhuman and sub-human, voracious, consuming and, in the end, consumed. 'The bond cracked 'twixt son and father' (I.2.108) signifies the disintegration of normality, of civilized convention, personal sanity and overall order. In such a society, the monsters find willing agents, like Oswald or the Captain at Edmund's order, and a Cordelia is doomed.

Yet as often in Shakespeare, another side is shown. Kent, Albany, France, the Fool, Cornwall's servant, exist, even though they do not triumph, to testify to a higher form of 'nature'. Their values are enhanced, not destroyed, by the play.

TL

Lear's daughters: three sisters

When the course team first discussed a contribution to this Forum on the women characters in *King Lear*, a colleague remarked, 'I never thought there was much to say about them except that one was good and the other two bad'. That they are so is indisputable and, the more I reflected on this fact, the greater became my conviction that this stark contrast is quite deliberate on Shakespeare's part and serves important purposes. They are not complex characters (like Edgar) but neither are they simply representations of 'good' and 'evil', as any good production will demonstrate. So, my discussion of these three sisters, the only women characters in the play, falls into two parts: in the first I shall consider them as two malign characters contrasted with one benign, in the second I shall examine Shakespeare's characterization of them in less abstract terms.

Regan, Gonerill, and Cordelia appear all together only once in the play—in the first scene—and Shakespeare avoids any later confrontation between Cordelia and her sisters, as events develop, for neither of the plot lines would be served by their meeting again. Whenever I see or read this first scene, I am irresistibly reminded of a children's story where there are three sisters, two bad and one good. It could be *Cinderella*, or even a variation on the final scene of *Rumpelstiltskin:* Cordelia is expected to produce the charmed words and fails whereupon the King bursts into a great rage. The very names of these women (though not, of course, Shakespeare's invention) suggest their natures: 'Gonerill' and 'Regan' both harsh-sounding, 'Cordelia' gentler in sound and suggestive of things of the heart (the Latin for heart is *cor*). In a production there is also their physical appearance and dress to provide important clues to their different natures. In the 1983 Michael Elliot TV production Regan and Gonerill were both made to look as imperious and conscious of their position as Cordelia was humble: they were dressed in darker colours with braided hair, she was in white, her hair falling to her shoulders behind her ears. And in the 1983 production by the Royal Shakespeare Company, Regan was played by the actress Jenny Agutter who described the costume designed for her by Robert Crowley as having 'no zips. Everything was tight and rigid and upright. It made me breathe from the top of my chest and that's where Regan should breathe from . . . I certainly couldn't slouch in Crowley's dress. And Regan should never slouch for a moment' (*Observer Magazine*, 18 December 1983, p. 42). Graham Martin has rightly brought to your attention the 'asides' that Cordelia makes before she is called on to speak, and pointed out that they are indications of her sincerity.

What else do they tell us about Cordelia's relationship to her sisters? Try to imagine how the scene might actually be *played* and think forward to the end where Cordelia makes her parting speech to her sisters.

To me, they indicate how shocked even she is at the gross flattery and hypocrisy of her sisters. Language is so tainted by the lying of her sisters that she resolves to 'be silent' and only replies at greater length when ordered to. In this speech ('Good my lord,/You have begot me . . . I.1.95–6) Regan and Gonerill are implicitly criticized for not loving their husbands, a charge which proves only too accurate in the light of later events, though we are not to know that at this stage. Nevertheless, at this early point, Cordelia emerges the clear moral victor in this scene. Her parting shots, 'I know you what you are' . . . (I.1.269), are a judgement on her sisters which is immediately vindicated by the discussion between them which brings the scene to a close. This concluding dialogue is important because it dispels any doubt at all about the 'love' that Regan and Gonerill bear Lear and leaves the audience with a clearly established and absolute divide between them and Cordelia.

There are two important purposes served by this unambiguous division, one structural and the other thematic. The structural usefulness is related to the overall design of the play, bearing in mind Lear's deterioration and later recovery. A symmetry emerges as the action develops. Regan and Gonerill are involved in Lear's descent into madness as is Cordelia in his recovery. As early as I.4, Lear shows signs of severe inner turmoil. Gonerill's behaviour causes him to question his own identity, and when he asks Gonerill 'Your name, fair gentlewoman?' (I.4.232), it is not, I think, a sarcastic question but genuine bewilderment. The process is completed by her collusion with Regan in III.4 which culminates in Lear's departure into the storm. After that, neither he nor Cordelia sees them again, for, by the time they are Edmund's prisoners in Act V, Gonerill has poisoned Regan and then committed suicide. This view of events suggests that the King is more of a victim than Graham Martin has proposed, when he stated that 'Lear is in large measure responsible for what happens to him' (see p. 16). I would argue, in any case, that Lear's initial act of folly and subsequent self-pity in no way diminish the wickedness of his daughters' treatment of him. It is true that his madness comes from within himself but, surely, it is events brought about by them which precipitate it?

Now look at IV.3, omitted from the Folio text and often from productions too, perhaps because it does not move the action forward. Yet it has none the less a genuine purpose in preparing for Lear and Cordelia's reunion. The gentleman describes her grief in language that suggests a religious dimension to her presence:

> . . . There she shook
> The *holy* water from her *heavenly* eyes,
> And clamour moistened . . .
>
> (IV.3.29–31)

For his part, Lear is described by Kent as suffering 'burning shame' at the memory of his treatment of his younger daughter so that when, in IV.7, they meet again, the emotional pitch of the reunion has been prepared for. Again, as Lear returns to sanity and consciousness, there is for me an effect of the ending of a fairy tale, though it is not to resemble one for long.

The 'thematic' purpose served by the uncompromising division of the sisters into 'good' and 'bad' takes us to the very heart of the play and involves some discussion of other characters, especially Kent and Edmund. Why these two?

Because they are the two characters, apart from the three sisters, who in my view are presented by Shakespeare as unambiguously 'good' and 'bad' respectively. If you think of I.1, Kent is the only person present, other than Cordelia, to put truth and loyalty first, whatever the cost, and it is he who helps her later in the 'healing' of her father. Likewise, Edmund's outright villainy proves him a fit suitor for either Regan or Gonerill, his only redeeming action being a last minute attempt to countermand his order to have Lear and Cordelia murdered, an act of clemency which he himself admits is 'Despite of mine own nature' (V.3.242). (Did Shakespeare realize that it was a little implausible?)

What is the 'thematic' purpose served by delineating these five characters in so morally unambiguous a fashion?

I would argue that one of Shakespeare's fundamental intentions in *King Lear* is to make his audience consider the nature of man himself and the ethics of his behaviour. By setting the play in a pagan world, he can do this free of the assumptions of a Christian society, yet the conclusions one is forced to draw are, in fact, the same as the teachings of the Church. Lear in his raving, for example, in upbraiding the imaginary 'rascal beadle' (IV.6.161 ff.) is essentially expounding Christ's teaching 'He who is without sin . . .' The need for values and a morality of behaviour, ideas which I shall come to in a moment, are starkly explored through the creation of characters of extreme good and wickedness. Lear, of course, doesn't fall into either category but then he *changes* in the course of the play. As Tony Lentin has pointed out (see p. 29) one of the major ideas Shakespeare explores in the play is the nature of filial duty and love, and again he does so by pairing and contrasts: Edmund is to Regan and Gonerill as Edgar is to Cordelia. Lear and Gloucester have in common the experience of being betrayed by one of their children and rescued by another. As far as Lear's children are concerned, it is in the first scene that principles for daughters are established and the difference in outlook between Cordelia and her sisters is expressed not only in what they say but also by the style of their speeches. Regan's and Gonerill's outrageous hyperbole is a rhetorical device, and there is nothing in what they say other than the obvious untruth that Lear is above all things to them. By contrast, Cordelia, finding herself unable to join in this contest, gives, when pressed, a reasoned and judicious account of her relationship with her father. (Graham Martin sees this scene as one in which a deadly game of politics is being played; it is possible, though, to perform Lear as a 'silly old fool' playing with his power, whereupon the scene can take on a slightly comic, though no less serious, dimension.) Notice how the words 'duty', 'duties' and 'bond' figure in it, and how Kent later commends Cordelia—she 'justly thinkst' and has 'most rightly said' (I.1.183). In performance, it is important for an actress to say Cordelia's lines here with some emotion, for otherwise they could make her appear unfeeling and merely dutiful. The important point that is made in these scenes is that relationships to fathers and husbands involve serious obligations as well as feelings and this has to be established early in the play because the results of a relationship based simply on feelings are soon to be made evident in the way that Regan and Gonerill treat their father.

> This brings me to the second part of my discussion: how much identity of their own do Regan, Gonerill and Cordelia have? Is it possible to say more than that one is 'good' and the two 'bad'? I would like you to think for a moment about the first confrontation (I.4) between Lear and Gonerill which results in his storming out of the palace. Is right entirely on his side in this scene?

The answer can hardly be a straightforward 'yes' or 'no'. Shakespeare has prepared for the confrontation in the previous scene where Gonerill and Oswald had been discussing Lear's tiresome habits as a guest .

> His knights have grown riotous, and himself upbraids us
> On every trifle.
>
> (I.3.7–8)

Notice that we have only Gonerill's report of this behaviour, we do not actually witness it and Lear denies it. Nevertheless, it is not difficult to see that there could well be some justification for her annoyance and this is dramatically necessary. It also makes Gonerill more convincing (she has some motive for her attitudes), though no less reprehensible, and judgement in the scene goes decidedly against her when Lear, amazed at the way she has addressed him, asks wonderingly 'Are you our daughter?' (I.4.214). Lear has thus reminded her of her filial status and it is this which renders her ingratitude so painful to him, not to speak of the *duty* which has been defined in I.1. The fourth commandment ('Honour thy father and thy mother') would have been very familiar to Shakespeare's audience, as would the further biblical injunction to make allowance for any infirmities of old age that parents display. As with the 'closet' scene in *Hamlet*, the parent–child relationship which touches a basic nerve in all of us is used to great effect by Shakespeare in creating a moment when every person in the audience can respond from his or her own experience. As Tony Lentin remarks, *we* are 'sons and daughters ourselves'.

The curse that Lear calls down on Gonerill and her womb is aimed directly at her female sexuality and her power herself to become a parent (ironically, because she would thus be spared his suffering). It calls to mind Lady Macbeth's invocation 'unsex me here . . .' when she resolves to murder Duncan. In both plays, resolution is seen as an attribute of masculinity, so Gonerill accuses Albany of 'milky gentleness' towards Lear (I.4.338) and, later, when he comes to Lear's defence, her supreme expression of contempt for him is 'Marry, your manhood! Mew!' (IV.2.68). In his speech 'O, reason not the need!' (II.4.259 ff.) Lear accuses his daughters of making him resort to 'women's weapons, water drops' (II.4.272) and his choice of adjective in denouncing them—'*unnatural* hags'—is significant, for there has been a reversal of the accepted gender roles. They in their scarcely credible cruelty are acting like men and he is reduced to playing the woman.

Another aspect of this role reversal is seen in the way the two women pursue Edmund in an openly lustful way. I can't think of another Shakespeare play where women of their social standing are so unashamedly keen to be adulteresses and rid of their husbands. (In Michael Elliot's 1983 TV production Cornwall does not 'Exit . . . supported by Regan' after his wounding in III.7 as the stage direction in your edition suggests but is simply left by her lying on the ground.) In this way, another contrast is set up between them and Cordelia who has made a genuine marriage in Act I. When Burgundy withdraws his offer on Lear's disinheriting her, her reply is, in effect, that she would not have had him anyway as he does not value her for herself:

> Peace be with Burgundy!
> Since that respect and fortunes are his love,
> I shall not be his wife.
>
> (I.1.247–9)

It is Cordelia, says the gentleman in IV.6, 'Who redeems nature from the general curse/Which twain have brought her to' (ll. 206–7), thus corresponding with Lear's condemnation of his other daughters as 'unnatural hags'.

I want to end by posing two questions about these characters put to me by fellow members of the course team.

---

(1) Is there *nothing* to be said in favour of Regan and Gonerill? Is the forcefulness of the latter in any way a quality to be respected?

(2) Why is Cordelia so insubstantial a character? It is this quality which would make a marriage between her and Edgar in the 'happy ending' version of the play by Nahum Tate improbable (see set text introduction, pp. 46–7).

In my view the answer to (1) has to be 'no'. It's the same question which arises in discussing Satan in Milton's *Paradise Lost*: can a quality like steadfastness be separated from the use to which it is put? In any reading of the play, Shakespeare does not intend Regan and Gonerill to be seen as other than wicked. Interestingly, the actress Judi Dench tried to play Regan as a more complex character but found that it 'didn't work and I was absolutely awful'.* In like manner, Shakespeare means Cordelia to embody dutifulness and self-sacrificing love, and 'good' characters are notoriously difficult to portray which perhaps explains (2). (Cicely Havely has more to say about Cordelia later in this block.) So, I would argue this 'black' and 'white' characterization is quite deliberate. These three women characters are not as complex or 'interesting' as Lear, Edmund or Edgar but they are vital to the exposition of Shakespeare's purposes in this moral tale.

RD

*Cook, Judith (1980) *Women in Shakespeare*, Harrap, p. 116.

Part Two
Interpretations

Introduction

IN this part of the block I am assuming that you are now reasonably familiar with the text of *King Lear* and in a position to engage on your own terms in critical debate about the play as a whole. But let us begin with what you decided was your overall impression of *King Lear*, the point which I hope was focussed by the list of quotations on page 27 above. Another way of trying to define this overall impression is to contrast the play with the other two tragedies studied in this course: *Hamlet*, written before *King Lear*, and *Antony and Cleopatra*, written after it.

Can you now make a short list of prominent features in *King Lear* which *distinguish* it from the other two tragedies?

There are, of course, very many points of comparison and contrast, and my short list is in no sense exemplary. But perhaps it will overlap to some degree with yours? And, if not, then do use the contradiction between us to defend your own, assembling more evidence for it from further reading of the play.

My first point is the pessimistic spirit of *King Lear*. (By 'pessimistic', I do not intend any elaborated philosophical position, but only the play's bleak representation of human life, and strikingly painful conclusion.) The contrast with *Antony and Cleopatra* is surely inescapable. Certainly, that play's hero and heroine come to grief but there are not the awful calamities which afflict Lear and his family and court. *Antony and Cleopatra* exudes a kind of sunny spaciousness, all its own. Human happiness, human pleasure, human achievement—the play may show their cost, the ambiguities attending upon their realization, but it also affirms them as realities. *King Lear*, and indeed *Hamlet*, are comparably very sombre plays. Do any of the characters show evidence of having *a good time?* The Gravedigger perhaps? Hamlet's occasional high spirits, his pleasure in wit and intrigue, seem always touched by an hysterical note, surely? Edmund? Oswald? The Fool? Any other candidates?

But then, while *Hamlet* is nearer in mood to *King Lear*, it is not an unreservedly gloomy play. Hamlet makes various comments about the ups-and-downs of human existence, but we link his more melancholy and critical judgements to his particular personal crisis. The speech celebrating human potentiality—'What a piece of work is a man . . .' (II.2.303 ff.)—is as characteristic of Hamlet as the famous soliloquy about reasons for and against suicide. However complexly we feel about the play's bloody conclusion, Claudius's death represents a kind of moral affirmation, and Hamlet's, though painful enough, doesn't prompt generalizing conclusions about the emptiness of human existence. The detective-story element also distinguishes *Hamlet* from *King Lear*, the sense of truth finally made manifest, of vice uncovered and virtue 'justified', even if not exactly triumphant. Difficult general questions are indeed raised ('for who *would* fardels bear?'), but they are not pressed to a conclusion. The play does not leave us wondering whether human life is worth having at all. And isn't that exactly the question which the conclusion of *King Lear* obliges us to ask?

My second point would be the *extreme* character of so many episodes in *King Lear*: the King cursing his daughters, his behaviour in Act III, Edgar's life as Poor Tom, the blinding of Gloucester, Cornwall's order to 'Turn out that eyeless villain' (III.7.95), Gloucester's 'suicide', his meeting with the mad King in IV.6, Cordelia's death, Lear's last speech. If we need confirmation that in *King*

Lear Shakespeare deliberately pushed issues to an extreme, we can cite the words prompted by Lear's appearance with the dead Cordelia in his arms.

> *Kent* Is this the promised end?
> *Edgar* Or image of that horror?
> *Albany* Fall and cease!
>
> (V.3.261–2)

What is 'the promised end'? Have you looked up the set-text editor's note here? And what do Albany's words mean? The general allusion is to the end of the world and the Last Judgement; and a play whose dénouement invites that analogy is surely extreme? The words themselves have the effect not so much of speeches from characters whom we know, as impersonal utterances, or as being quasi-musical, resembling the final reprise of some key motif in a Mahler symphony, sombre, lucid and unanswerable. Don't these brief reverberating exchanges amongst the appalled survivors summarize the play's dominant note? Is there anything of this kind in *Hamlet* ('Let four captains/Bear Hamlet like a soldier to the stage' (V.2.389–90)), or in *Antony and Cleopatra* ('Now boast thee, death, in thy possession lies/A lass unparalleled' (V.2.315–6))? Lear in one of his raging curses bids the thunder to

> Crack Nature's moulds, all germens spill at once
> That makes ingrateful man!
>
> (III.2.8–9)

The play, as a whole, lives up to the spirit of such words.

My third candidate for a short list of *King Lear's* distinctive features would be the play's 'metaphysical' character. Most Shakespeare plays have a questioning 'philosophical' element, even the comedies. *Hamlet*, of course, is such a play. *Antony and Cleopatra*? On the whole, I would call it the least 'philosophical' of the tragedies. *King Lear* differs from the others, however, in organizing the whole action round large general questions from whose implications none of the characters escapes. Thus, when Lear says: 'Then let them anatomize Regan, see what breeds about her heart. Is there any cause in nature that makes these hard hearts?' (III.6.75–7), that second question widens the issue to include *all* hardness of heart, in any place and at any time. Edgar, having survived the storm scenes in Act III, congratulates himself on having touched the nadir of life. He then sees approaching his blinded father, forcing him to admit that 'The worst is not,/So long as we can say "This is the worst".' (IV.1.27–8). Albany, hearing of Gonerill and Regan's treatment of their father, exclaims that if such behaviour goes unpunished by 'the heavens', then 'Humanity must perforce prey on itself/Like monsters of the deep' (IV.2.46–9). The play's events push the characters towards such generalizing remarks, conclusions and questionings, as if that indeed were Shakespeare's overriding purpose in dramatizing the story. Or take this curt military exchange when Edmund instructs one of his captains to kill Lear and Cordelia.

> *Edmund* About it; and write happy when th' hast done.
> Mark, I say 'instantly'; and carry it so
> As I have set it down.
> *Captain* I cannot draw a cart nor eat dried oats;
> If it be man's work, I'll do't.
>
> (V.3.36–40)

Is the execution of Lear and Cordelia *man's* work? The Captain decides that it is. So is the implication that *man*, as a species, is to be distinguished from the cart-drawing and oat-eating *horse* by the fact that he kills the helpless and the innocent?

That is the *kind* of question the play keeps asking—and not answering. In describing such questions as 'metaphysical' or 'philosophical', I do not mean to imply that Shakespeare raises them in an abstract, or merely discursive way. Always, they emerge out of particular human actions, rendered within a particular human situation. Indeed, in leaving them as questions Shakespeare may be said to ensure that they do not escape the particularizing effect of the events that provoke them.

One reader's individual impressions of any work as substantial, challenging and complex as *King Lear* are, of course, all too likely to strike another as arbitary and tendentious. But I think you can agree that the three features of *King Lear* which I have chosen receive some support from the text. In any case, the point of the exercise has been to encourage you to formulate your own general sense of the play, as a basis for considering some leading interpretations which we will now look at, selected, it must at once be added, from a mass of commentary, and without any claim to represent its wealth or variety.

Is King Lear *a 'religious' play?*

There are two main reasons for beginning with this question. One is the considerable body of commentary on *King Lear* permeated by the notion that it *is* a 'religious' play. We shall discuss such views shortly. But the other reason may be conveniently mentioned at once. Contemporary description of the play as 'tragedie' (its title in the First Folio (1623) printing of Shakespeare's *œuvre*) or of the older *King Leir* as a 'tragecall history' (the entry in the Stationer's Register, an official record where every published book was supposed to be listed) could be taken to imply a 'religious' dimension. If you glance back at Cicely Havely's account of the dramatic tradition within which Shakespeare worked (Block II, pp. 91–2), you will see that 'tragedy' usually meant a tale about the misfortunes of royal or noble persons. An important source of such tales was the collection by Boccaccio entitled *De casibus virorum illustrium*, translated into English by the Benedictine monk John Lydgate in a spirit of gloomy conscientiousness, as *Falls of Princes* (1494). Such tales were held to point to a simple moral, particularly satisfying (we may suppose) if the reader were neither Prince nor Princess nor laid claim to being one of the 'virorum illustrium'. They narrated thoroughgoing reversals of wordly fortune—riches to rags—illustrating in copious detail the view that human prosperity was inherently unstable, and that human achievements, however splendid from the secular point of view, however linked with the impressive attributes of royal aristocratic families, were of no account in the sight of God. Dame Fortune, or perhaps rather we should say, Dame Misfortune dealing out pains, tribulations and diseases to everybody, regardless of rank or position, enforced this divine view of the worthlessness, as well as of the sinful character, of secular human life. According to that favourite metaphor of medieval thinking, the Wheel of Fortune drew individuals up to glory, and then by the same inexorable movement pulled them down into catastrophe. In this spirit, Sir Walter Ralegh, composing his *History of the World* (1614) in the Tower of London, indirectly meditating his own case, wrote these sentences:*

> If we truly examine the difference of both conditions; to wit of the rich and mighty, whom we call fortunate; and of the poor and oppressed, whom we account wretched: we shall find the happiness of the one, and the miserable estate of the other, so tied by God to the very instant, and both so subject to interchange (witness the sudden downfall of the greatest princes, and the speedy rising up of the meanest persons) as the one hath nothing so certain, whereof to bewail itself. For there is no man

* Cited in Reese, M. M. (1961) *The Cease of Majesty*, Arnold, p. 17.

> so assured of his honour, of his riches, health, or life, but that he may be deprived of either or all, the very next hour or day to come.

And he goes on to add in a memorable metaphor:

> God, who is the author of all our tragedies, hath written out for us, and appointed us all the parts we are to play: and hath not, in their distribution been partial to the most mighty princes of the world.

In Part Three, we will be discussing the question of 'tragedy' more fully, but it is clear that what we might call the baseline definition, common in Shakespeare's day, has its application to *King Lear.* Most of its highly-placed personages fall from high position and die (Lear, Gloucester, Cornwall, Regan, Gonerill, Kent). Edmund both rises and falls in a manner that perfectly illustrates the logic of Fortune's Wheel. So can the play be seen to deliver the kind of lesson indicated in the quotations from Sir Walter Ralegh—pointing out the vanity of human ambitions in the sight of God? Here we must recognize that the term 'religious' could only mean 'Christian' for Shakespeare and his audience. So our question at once raises the issue of whether Shakespeare intended the play to reflect Christian ideas, or like its source material, to portray a pre-Christian society. As we have seen from its inclusion in *The Chronicles of England, Scotlande, and Irelande*, compiled by Raphael Holinshed, and, as you know, quarried by Shakespeare for several History plays about the pre-Tudor period, the Lear story was accepted as *true*, in the way that Sir Thomas More's *History of Richard III* (1513) was accepted as the truth about that monarch. Now Holinshed dates Lear's reign 'in the year of the world 3105' long before the birth of Christ.

Look back at the play's first scene for suggestions that Shakespeare wanted the audience to think of a pre-Christian society.

I hope you noticed two at least pieces of evidence. When Lear utters his rejection of Cordelia (I.1.108–20), he swears by pagan deities: the sun, 'The mysteries of Hecat and the night'—goddess of the moon and of witchcraft, and by the stars; and when he and Kent argue, both invoke Apollo (I.1.160).

But is this just for the sake of a first impression? Is the rest of the play consistent with this pre-Christian emphasis? On page 27, I asked you to consider some quotations as to their representative character for the play as a whole. Look back at them now. How do some of them bear upon the question we are discussing here?

In (3) Albany speaks of 'the heavens' and of 'visible spirits', where the analogous Christian ideas would be 'Heaven', and perhaps 'angels', or at any rate 'messengers from God'. Albany's words might be thought of as vague pagan imitations of Christian ideas, but not more. The other quotations all refer to 'the gods', and while specific references to 'God' in stage plays was officially frowned upon, these 'gods' can hardly be thought of as a censored version of 'God'. Their relation to human life is far too unclear. Is Gloucester in (2) right about them, or Edgar in (4)? Does the stage direction in (5) that follows Albany's 'The gods defend her' imply that they are incapable of doing so, or just unwilling? Elsewhere, Gloucester speaks of 'You ever-gentle gods' (IV.6.217), and Cordelia prays to 'you kind gods' (IV.7.14) to cure her father's madness. The only thing certain about 'the gods' in *King Lear* is that, invoked on all hands, and characterized in several different ways (just, indifferent, kind, maleficent, helpless, or merely refusing to help), they remain enigmatic. And to this we may add the deliberate juxtaposition of Gloucester's superstitious belief that human events are influenced by solar and lunar eclipses with Edmund's scornful rejection of such ideas (I.2.103–36). Astrology was widely believed in Shakespeare's times, and Edmund's vigorous contempt could be that of a contemporary intellectual sceptic. (Edmund, as we shall see, invokes 'Nature', not any god; he could be called the play's materialist.)

The general impression emerging from these examples would suggest that Shakespeare had in mind a pre-Christian society, having a conception of powerful deities whom prayer might, or might not, persuade to intervene in human affairs. The contrast with the Christian monotheistic conception of 'God' with his elaborate if also puzzling plan for humankind is evident enough. Yet there *are* references to Christian thinking. It is said of Cordelia that she 'redeems nature from the general curse' which the behaviour of Gonerill and Regan has brought down (IV.6.206). The set-text editor points out that there are two levels of meaning here. Gonerill and Regan have brought down a 'curse' on Britain by contributing to its political divisions. But also, the lines refer to the Fall of Man brought about by Adam and Eve's disobedience, a 'general curse' from which Christ eventually redeemed both humankind and Nature. Cordelia thus becomes 'a Christ-like redeeming figure' (set text, page 293). This Christian allusion is reinforced when Lear, waking from curative sleep and supposing himself to have died and gone to hell, greets Cordelia as a 'soul in bliss' (IV.7.46), while in his speech to Cordelia after their capture by Edmund's soldiers, he envisages a life with her in prison 'As if we were God's spies' (V.3.17), which the editor accepts as monotheistic despite the non-pagan implications (set text, page 302). Then, in the last scene, we find allusions to the *Gospel according to St Mark*, when Kent, Edgar and Albany compare the sight of Lear with the dead Cordelia in his arms (V.3.261–3) with the end of the world as described by Christ to his disciples. In this respect, the three noblemen would seem to speak, not as members of a pre-Christian society, but as Shakespeare's contemporaries who possess a good knowledge of the Bible.

But whatever is to be made of these passing allusions to Christian thought, and some commentators think them crucial, they do little to counter the general effect of a world with only very vague religious ideas. The notable *absence*, in this respect, is of any clerical personages, of the Christian Church as an institution, or of references to Christian religious practice. (Contrast the *Henry IV* plays, with their 'political' clerics, or in *Hamlet*, Ophelia's burial, or in *Measure for Measure*, the religious order Isabella plans to join.) So it is surely clear that *King Lear* contains no general lesson about the 'Fall of Princes' and the unstable character of human achievements or qualities such as would have fitted the traditional conception held by Sir Walter Ralegh. If we are looking for a straight-forward lesson which the first night *King Lear* audience *might* have drawn from the play, it would be more on the lines of 'just what you might expect from a society lacking the benefit of the Christian revelation'. And this point can be put in a more positive way. Characters in *King Lear* do believe in 'gods', and repeatedly invoke their help. What is also evident is that direct help is unavailable. In the storm scenes, Lear invites the gods to take his part. Do they? Lear is helped, if helped at all, by Kent and Gloucester. Cordelia prays that the gods may cure him. What the play shows are human remedies—herbal cures, sleep, kindness, above all his discovery that Cordelia offers no accusations or blame. Gloucester's view of the gods, as is consistent with his superstitious nature, alters as a result of Edgar's remedial attention. Before the suicide attempt, Gloucester thinks the gods are cruelly detached spectators who 'kill us for their sport' (IV.1.37); afterwards, he finds them 'ever-gentle' (IV.6.217). Albany's request that the gods 'defend' Cordelia (V.3.254) is answered by the entry of Lear carrying her dead body. We may say, then, that people in this play appeal to 'the gods' as a way of articulating their feelings about an insoluble crisis, an imminent catastrophe, or some awful recognition about the reality of their lives. As a term and a concept 'the gods' in *King Lear* can be said to be (to quote T. S. Eliot) 'a way of putting it—not very satisfactory', where 'it' represents the crisis, or catastrophe, or painful discovery of an unalterable truth. In *King Lear* 'the gods' solve *nothing*. However much they exist in the minds of the characters, as effective agents in the play 'supernatural values' are strikingly absent. 'Values' inhere in, are constructed by, are challenged, destroyed, recovered, transformed by, human actors in recognizably human deeds.

We may note also Shakespeare's brilliance in having constructed this subtly ambiguous fictional world for Lear's situation. It is not pre-Christian in such a way that its audience would think it *entirely* alien (the kind of world invented, say, by William Golding in *The Inheritors* about a pacific and vegetarian human species which loses its Darwinian struggle for survival with an early version of *homo sapiens:* aggressive, carnivorous, and hierarchical). The scatter of allusions to Christian ideas ensures a certain familiarizing effect. And a further instance of this ambiguity is powerfully *theatrical*: the use of thunder. The onset of Lear's mental crisis is announced, you will recall, by a stage direction 'storm and tempest' (II.4.279), and Lear's defiance of the elements described in III.1, and shown in III.2 is accompanied by 'storm still', the stage direction which prefaces each of these scenes. Now the stage convention of the period was that thunder represented divine displeasure; the actual noise emanated from the canopy which stretched over the stage and was known as 'the heavens'. (See Professor Gurr's discussion of the Elizabethan–Jacobean theatre on Cassette 1.) So, the thunder that Lear both appeals to and defies as 'elements' (III.2.16) could be read in two ways: as a merely natural phenomenon, in which case Lear's imprecations belong to the superstitious practices of a pre-Christian society, both pitiful and ludicrous; yet also as the sign of a Christian God's wrath at Lear's disastrous mistakes. This double-edged effect leaves an imaginative 'space' for the further conception that the storm is an objectification of Lear's mental turmoil, and as we have seen in our earlier discussion of his madness, this is where Shakespeare's interest really lies.

In setting aside a Ralegh-like response to *King Lear*, we have by no means exhausted our topic. Some Greek tragedy, for example, depends upon a religious framework, and as a colleague on the course team pointed out, so does the Book of Job. Yet no simple moral lessons can be derived from such examples. So let us now approach more recent religious, indeed Christian, interpretations of *King Lear* by looking at a particular issue which is surely central to the play: the death of Cordelia.

Lear and the dead Cordelia, V.3: 'Howl, howl, howl! O, you are men of stones!' line 255. (Kozintsev's King Lear.) *(Courtesy of National Film Archive/Stills Library)*

Why does Cordelia die?

In 1681, a Restoration dramatist called Nahum Tate (1652–1715) produced for the stage an adapted version of *King Lear*, which proved popular. Please now read the Preface to the set text (pages 47–9), which gives an account of Tate's version. Then consider this comment of Dr Johnson on these changes, taken from the 1765 edition of the plays:

> *Shakespeare* has suffered the virtue of Cordelia to perish in a just cause, contrary to the natural ideas of justice, to the hope of the reader, and, what is yet more strange, to the faith of chronicles. Yet this conduct is justified by the Spectator [a periodical edited by Joseph Addison], who blames Tate for giving Cordelia success and happiness in his alteration, and declares, that, in his opinion, *the tragedy has lost half its beauty* . . . A play in which the wicked prosper, and the virtuous miscarry, may doubtless be good, because it is a just representation of the common events of human life: but since all reasonable beings naturally love justice, I cannot easily be persuaded, that the observation of justice makes a play worse; or, that if the other excellencies are equal, the audience will not always rise better pleased from the final triumph of persecuted virtue.
>
> In the present case, the publick has decided. *Cordelia*, from the time of *Tate*, has always retired with victory and felicity. And if my sensations could add anything to the general suffrage, I might relate, that I was many years ago so shocked by Cordelia's death that I know not whether I ever endured to read again the last scenes of the play till I undertook to revise them as an editor.*

As a critic of literature, Johnson has an entirely undeserved reputation for inflexible pronouncements which leave no room for further discussion. Here, as you can see, he is evidently torn in two opposite directions.

What are the two conflicting arguments he is unable to resolve? And what is your own view of the substantial issue (Cordelia's death)? Would Shakespeare's play be *radically* altered if we envisage—nothing so drastic as Tate's reworking of his Shakespearian source—but merely a last-moment rescue of Lear and Cordelia from the soldier appointed by Edmund to kill them? Work out your reasons for the opinion you come to.

Johnson's account turns on the conflict between two ideas. One is that good plays should be 'a just representation of the common events of human life', and a play in which 'the wicked prosper and the virtuous miscarry' is *precisely that.* The second is that 'all reasonable beings naturally love justice', and a good play should, in its denouement, recognize this. So, Tate's version is less true to life, but meets our natural love of justice, while Shakespeare's version is more true to life, but offends against our natural love of justice. Johnson leaves the issue open, and though the way he discusses the point may not be ours, doesn't he succeed in pinpointing its importance?

Indeed, Shakespeare's construction of the scene which concludes in the *coup de théâtre* of Lear's final entry forces the issue upon us. V.3 begins with Lear and Cordelia captured, and Edmund's instruction to his Captain to have them killed. Then follows Edgar's challenge to Edmund, their fight, and Edmund's defeat, Edgar's lengthy account of his father's death and its effect on Kent, the news of Gonerill's suicide, Kent's arrival, the showing of the dead bodies of the two sisters, and finally Edmund's confession that his 'writ/Is on the life of Lear and on Cordelia' (V.3.243–4), but that there may still be time to save them.

*Raleigh, Walter, *op. cit.*, pp. 161–2.

'Enter in conquest with drum and colours Edmund; Lear and Cordelia as prisoners; soldiers, Captain', *V.3*. (*Kozintsev's* King Lear.) (*Courtesy of National Film Archive/Stills Library*)

Shakespeare's ability to keep the audience on tenterhooks is nowhere better illustrated than here! For with the 'happy ending' effected by Edgar's victory over Edmund, the wicked sisters dead, the virtuous survivors (Albany, Kent, Edgar) all assembled, a 'nick-of-time' rescue for Lear and Cordelia is perfectly conceivable. Yet Shakespeare chose differently, so surely he intends the effect of *shock* wrought upon Dr Johnson? Lear's entry, Cordelia in his arms, contrives one of those *extreme* effects that I suggested are characteristic of the play, and the construction of the scene shows that such an effect was carefully planned for. So would the play be *radically* altered if Cordelia had survived? What did you decide? Her death by hanging, the least deserved of the calamities in this play, is clearly in tune with its general mood. But don't we need some further justification? Even if Cordelia had survived, the rest of the play would still be pretty grim.

> Is Shakespeare merely complying with Johnson's sense of truth-to-life that usually 'the virtuous miscarry'? Has he some further or different purpose beyond providing yet another painful shock to the feeling of his audience? What were your thoughts about this?

This is the point when we can consider the Christian assumption which affects some twentieth-century thinking about *King Lear*. In Block II, Cicely Havely mentioned the work of the influential critic A. C. Bradley, discussing his comments on *Antony and Cleopatra*. Much of Bradley's thinking has, as she says, dated, but his views remain influential, partly because of the thoroughness of his immersion in the plays he discusses, and in respect of *King Lear*, we have a case in point. Bradley gave a set of lectures which were published as *Shakespearean Tragedy* (1905), and those on *King Lear* proposed that the essence of Shakespeare's play could be called 'The Redemption of Lear'.* The play shows Lear discovering through bitter humiliation and rending pain the extent of his own initial folly, and the true character of each of his three daughters. At first driven by the desire for revenge upon the 'pelican daughters' (III.4.72), the fierce need to inflict pain on those who have caused him pain, he wakes from restorative sleep to learn that the much-injured Cordelia feels no such passion against him. On the contrary, she wants only to bind up the wounds, to heal and restore. During the storm

*Bradley, A. C. (1957) *Shakespearean Tragedy*, Macmillan, p. 253.

scenes, he discovered truths about the poor and down-trodden, releasing in him an impulse of fellow-feeling for their condition, and about the real working of legal authority and the hollowness of human 'justice'. It is his sufferings that teach Lear all this, and (to cite the conclusion of Bradley's encomium):*

> [his] sight is so purged by scalding tears that it sees at last how power and place and all things in the world are vanity except love; [he] tastes in his last hours the extremes both of love's rapture and of its agony, but could never, if he lived on or lived again, care a jot for aught beside—there is no figure, surely, in the world of poetry at once so grand, so pathetic, and so beautiful as this.

As you can see from these words, by 'The Redemption of King Lear' Bradley means that he has been, not just morally improved by his sufferings, but spiritually *redeemed* from the vanities of all worldly life, and he cites Lear's speech to Cordelia about the life they will live in prison (V.3.8–19) as supporting the view that, finally, he *has* renounced all secular values.

Important in his argument is a particular reading of Lear's last speech. Bradley proposes that Lear, *believing Cordelia still lives,* himself dies in an ecstasy of joy.†

Would you now look up the speech (V.3.303–9), and consider Bradley's view?

Did you find it a persuasive reading?—'Do you see this? Look on her! Look, her lips!/Look there! Look there!', followed by the stage direction '*He dies*'. The point still remains, of course, how this affects us. Bradley concedes as much when he adds:¶

> To us perhaps, the knowledge that he is deceived may bring a culmination of pain.

His main point is that whatever we may think of it, Lear's joy is real to him, that like Gloucester he dies 'smilingly', and that this is, as it were, the spiritual consequence and reward of his renunciation of worldly values. Bradley then takes up the question of Cordelia's death, which he accounts for in two ways. The first‡ somewhat resembles Johnson's appeal to experience.

> . . . this destruction of the good through the evil of others is one of the tragic facts of life, and no one can object to the use of it, within certain limits, in tragic art.

Cordelia's death belongs to 'the nature of things'. Or as Johnson puts it, life teaches us that commonly 'the virtuous miscarry'. But it is Bradley's second argument§ that we need to isolate. Cordelia is in her own right a heroic spirit who embodies an essential feature of Shakespearean tragedy. She displays a greatness of soul enabling her to rise above the world in which she suffers.

> . . . what happens to such a being does not matter; all that matters is what she is . . . The more unmotived, unmerited, senseless, monstrous her fate, the more do we feel it does not concern her . . . The judgement of this world is a lie; its goods, which we covet, corrupt us; its ills,

**Idem,* p. 235.
†*Idem,* p. 241.
¶*Idem,* p. 241.
‡*Idem,* p. 270.
§*Idem,* p. 272–3.

> which break our bodies, set our souls free . . . Let us renounce the world, hate it, and lose it gladly. The only real thing in it is the soul, with its courage, patience, devotion. And nothing outward can touch that.

Notice how Bradley moves from analysis to rhetoric! Cordelia's death teaches us that the world is nothing, and the soul everything ('Let us renounce the world' etc.). The phrasing here may be usefully set beside one of Christ's utterances to his disciples:

> For what is a man profited, if he shall gain the whole world, and lose his own soul? or what shall a man give in exchange for his soul?
>
> (Matthew 16: 26)

I think we can see that Bradley's argument about Lear and Cordelia is, in fact, suffused with an implicit Christianity. Lear and Cordelia jointly affirm a 'contempt of the world' which, with whatever qualifications, it is always the business of Christian teaching to convey. The question which his account, however, ignores is the insistent presence in *King Lear* of that very 'worldliness' which Lear and Cordelia leave behind, so that as audience, we respond to their fates as only one element in that more complex design. Bradley gives them an undue prominence because he holds to the notion of *King Lear* as resembling a *poem* to be read and pondered in the imagination, rather than as a *drama* to be staged. He abstracts from the dense and intertwined dramatic tissue of the final scene the *internal* emotions of Lear (joy) and Cordelia (Christian stoic detachment), and treats them as dominant. Such an analysis simply forgets the carefully calculated *stage shock* brought about by Lear's entry with Cordelia's body, as it forgets the sombre end-of-the-world responses of Edgar, Kent and Lear, which in a dramatic version the audience cannot but see and hear. Moreover, the play ends with an insistent reminder that, however 'worldly' the world may be judged, *it will not go away.* 'Friends of my soul, you twain,' says Albany to Edgar and Kent, 'Rule in this realm, and the gored state sustain' (V.3.317–8). In sum the problems of the state which Lear's (and others') actions have so thoroughly 'gored' remain to be addressed.

It is nevertheless fair to add that a Christian view of *King Lear* has been argued in a more intensive and sustained manner than Bradley's. If you want to pursue the issue, you could consult Parker's *The Slave of Life**, in which Cordelia is seen as 'an analogue' for Christ in a pagan world, and the play is called 'a Calvary without a resurrection' (p. 142). J. C. Maxwell has called *King Lear* 'a Christian play about a pagan world'.† Some commentators, agreeing with Bradley's view that Lear dies in the belief that Cordelia is alive, perceive a symbolic truth in his delusion. This view is elaborated by Siegel in *Shakespeare in his Time and Ours*, who perceives a pattern in Shakespeare's work as a whole of 'kneeling-resurrection'.¶

> In view of the fact that kneeling in *King Lear* consistently accompanies happenings that bear the aspect of miracle, this conjunction of kneeling and resurrection—a resurrection which is also presented as rebirth—is surely significant.

Siegel's general thesis is that Shakespeare's tragedies were an expression of the 'Christian humanism that dominated the thought of the time'.‡ Chapter 2 of his book puts this case.

*Parker, M. D. H. (1955) *The Slave of Life*, Chatto & Windus, chap. 4.
†Cited Muir, K. (ed.) (1952) *King Lear*, The Arden Shakespeare, Methuen, p. lvi.
¶Siegel, Paul N. (1968) *Shakespeare in his Time and Ours*, University of Notre Dame Press, pp. 112–13.
‡*Idem*, p. 23.

'Nature' in King Lear

The second account of the play that I want now to consider makes extensive use of contemporary Elizabethan and Jacobean thinking about 'Nature', a concept which you may have noticed appears a good deal in the text.

For a brief initial exercise, turn first to Edmund's soliloquy (I.2.1–22), to Gloucester's speech to Edmund (I.2.103–7), and to Lear's speech to Regan (II.4.165–76). Each speech makes the term 'nature' central to the argument put forward by the different characters. But 'nature' does not always mean the same thing in these speeches. See if you can write brief definitions in each case. You won't need to consult a dictionary, the speeches themselves, together with the editorial notes, will provide enough material.

Edmund's speech appeals to an idea of 'Nature' prior to the social world in which legal concepts like 'base' and 'legitimate' have purchase. Defined as a 'bastard', born outside of the marriage law, Edmund asks this 'nature' to take his part, and such a phrase as 'the lusty stealth of *nature*' suggests an animal-like predatory quality. Your editor comments that Edmund's idea here 'lays stress on those endowments that prompts life in its most primitive conditions, nature red in tooth and claw' (set text, p. 198).

Gloucester's speech to Edmund invokes different ideas altogether. 'The King falls from bias of *nature*: there's father against child'. 'Nature' here refers to human loyalties and values. But, in 'the wisdom of *nature* can reason it thus and thus, yet *nature* find itself scourged by the sequent effects' the first example means something like 'reason' (explanations for the eclipses that are worrying Gloucester), and the second is the world of human and social obligations, as in 'bias of nature'.

Lear's speech to Regan invokes again the idea of 'nature' as a norm for human values: 'the offices of nature' include, for Lear, 'bond of childhood, effects of courtesy, dues of gratitude'.

In sum, there are three meanings: (a) the pre-social appetite for survival and dominance, (b) reason, or scientific knowledge, and (c) a nexus of social and personal values which enable us correctly to judge human actions.

How did you get on? You should certainly have arrived at definitions *resembling* these, if only by consulting the editorial notes on the speeches! (One note also refers you to pages 17–18 in the Introduction, which briefly surveys the meanings of 'Nature' in the play.) But what do these definitions have to do with the play as a whole? In discussing earlier some prominent features of *King Lear* I pointed to its 'metaphysical' tone. John F. Danby, a critic who drew attention to this in *Shakespeare's Doctrine of Nature: A Study of 'King Lear'* proposes that the play is constructed in terms of conflicting contemporary conceptions of 'Nature'. Partly this is an attempt to correct the earlier Bradleyan emphasis on individual character study, partly to challenge a preoccupation with the 'poetry' of the plays conceived as in some sense autonomous, a sphere of abstract patterning by means of recurrent imagery, disengaged from 'meaning', from Shakespeare's intellectual and moral engagement with the cultural and historical issues of his day. In proposing that *King Lear* is more a play of 'ideas' than of 'character', Danby correctly reminds us that differences over the meanings of words are, or can be, the opposite of dry abstract intellectual debate.

> Quarrels over what 'Nature' really means are not merely verbal: weapons will out as often as words. People identify themselves with the fate of their meaning. The quarrel might be a matter of life and death. Thus Giovanni Bruno was imprisoned in 1593 and burnt in 1600. One reason for this was an unacceptable sense in which he used the word 'Nature'.*

*Danby, John F. (1949) *Shakespeare's Doctrine of Nature: A Study of 'King Lear'*, Faber edn. (1968), pp. 15–16.

For a contemporary case, we might think of the fierce and deadly quarrels over the meaning of 'democracy' which have left their visible mark on the geography of contemporary Europe. To have a serious personal stake in a complex idea involves definitions, both of the world, and of the self, which cannot lightly face the challenge of alternative definitions. 'Coming out of me', wrote Auden, 'living is always thinking,/Thinking changing and changing living'.* This, in effect, is the kind of relationship that 'ideas' have to 'characters' in *King Lear*, most notably 'ideas' involving Nature.

Danby conceives the play as a 'thinking-through' of the clash between two main competing versions of 'Nature': Lear's, which is also Gloucester's, Kent's, Edgar's, and Albany's; as against Edmund's, which is also Gonerill's and Regan's. The first idea of 'Nature' draws, according to Danby, on an orthodoxy of Elizabethan thought, expressed in the philosophical and theological writings of such as Francis Bacon (1561–1626) in *The Advancement of Learning* (1605), and of Richard Hooker (?1554–1600) in *Of the Laws of Ecclesiastical Polity* (1593–7) which provided the Elizabethan establishment of the Anglican Church with its theological justification and defence. In these writings:†

> The idea of Nature . . . is always something normative for human beings. It is impossible to talk about Nature without talking also about pattern and ideal form; about Reason as displayed in Nature; about Law as the innermost expression of Nature; about Custom which is the basis of Law and equally with Law as an expression of Nature's pattern; about Restraint as the observance of Law, and the way to discover our richest self-fulfilment . . . [this] orthodox and benignant view . . . [is held by] those in the play who seem already to be slightly old-fashioned, but who are nevertheless unquestionably the most human.

'Nature' to Lear, as to those who side with him, signifies an interwoven structure of moral, social and political loyalties, which are *constitutive* of, that is to say, they define, what it is to be a normal human being. Gonerill and Regan are 'unnatural hags' (II.4.273) because they do not behave to their *father* 'naturally', with obedience, solicitude, kindness, just as they no longer grant him the privileges and deference due to a *king*. Lear's denunciation of both Cordelia and Gonerill (I.1.108–20, I.4.272–86), takes on a quasi-religious note. He invokes, as might a priest, the curse of a goddess who is the fount of the 'natural' values outraged (apparently) by Cordelia, (actually) by Gonerill. Lear asks the Fool, 'Who is it that can tell me who I am?' (I.4.226) because his conception of himself as father and absolute ruler has been challenged at the root by the behaviour of the 'unnatural daughters'. Outside the structure of political and social interconnections which he calls 'Nature', Lear *has* no identity—not at least till he constructs a different one. That is what his 'madness' means. His departure from the kind of habitation represented by the castles of Gonerill or Gloucester, where he had an acknowledged place, is a topographical version of his banishment from the structure of 'Nature'. Wind, storm and rain, an empty heath, represent his state of mind exactly. So, too, when he intends to strip off his clothes, we should recognize that these are not just material coverings, they signify his place within the 'natural' scheme of things. We remember that robes have a hierarchical and political meaning ('Thou are a lady', he says to Regan, noting her fine clothes (II.4.262)), and those without them are the poor and vagrant. In Lear's conception of 'Nature', the poor had their place, and he had duties of charity towards them. When he says 'O, I have ta'en/Too little care of this' (III.4.32–3), he recognizes that he has not discharged this 'natural' obligation. And we should remember that in cutting off Cordelia he offended directly against the 'natural' order which fathers and daughters should preserve in relation to each other, just as Gonerill and Regan

*Auden, W. H. (1966) *Collected Shorter Poems 1927–1957*, Faber, p. 35.
†Danby, *op. cit.*, p. 21.

offended against it. The process of events which makes Lear impotently invoke 'Nature' in his defence against his daughters' treatment was thus set going by his own act. His greeting of Poor Tom—'Thou art the thing itself!' (III.4.103)—represents his attempt to develop a new idea of 'human nature' outside the traditional structure. Instead of clothes, nakedness; instead of social obligations and relationships, solititude; instead of houses, heathland and storm; instead of 'humanity', a 'bare forked *animal*'.

I will leave you to pursue the parallel state of affairs in the case of Gloucester (Hunter's Introduction is helpful here, see the set text, pp. 18–22) since the thematic and conceptual link between the Lear and Gloucester plots is provided by a common reference to 'Nature'. And this brings us directly to Edmund. In Danby's argument, Edmund is the principal voice for a different idea about 'Nature', and in the clash between the two ideas, we find the illustration of Danby's insistence that 'different views of Nature . . . are not differences of opinion only. They are felt as so many stubborn holds that reality has on us and we on it'.* Edmund's 'Nature' is the term that validates a thrusting competitive individualism before which all shared values must give way. Danby suggests that the political philosopher, Thomas Hobbes (1588–1679) in his *Leviathan* (1651) offers the most explicit account of this different view of 'Nature', which had been gaining ground during the sixteenth century, and would certainly have been familiar to Shakespeare's audiences. Hobbes argued† that

> in the nature of man, we find three principal causes of quarrel. First, competition; secondly diffidence [i.e. suspicion, mistrust]; thirdly, glory. The first maketh man invade for gain; the second for safety; and the third for reputation . . . Hereby it is manifest that during the time men live without a common power to keep them all in awe, they are in that condition which is called war; and such a war, as is of every man, against every man . . . continual fear and danger of violent death; and the life of man, solitary, poor, nasty, brutish, and short.

'Nature' is not an encompassing structure within which human life achieves mutually beneficent satisfactions, but rather resembles Darwin's account of the natural world of a myriad living species competing against each other in a fierce struggle for survival.

It is interesting in this connection that in both Folio and Quarto texts of *King Lear* the usual name used for Edmund is 'Bastard' (set text, p. 322), and this is how he introduces himself to us in his soliloquy. He totally rejects the social and moral structure of 'Nature', to which Gloucester later appeals when he calls Edmund a 'Loyal and natural boy' (II.1.83). Notice the irony in that 'natural', which means to Gloucester loyalty but to Edmund offers a perfect justification for *treachery*. From the angle provided by Edmund's 'Nature' Gloucester's 'Nature' is a system of self-delusion which any tolerably clever and talented individual can profit by. And we see Edmund profiting, first by using Gloucester's idea of 'Nature' as a way of getting rid of Edgar, then himself when confided in by Gloucester over the letter about Cordelia's army (III.3.8–13), immediately betraying his 'natural' loyalty to a father by telling Cornwall. Where for Gloucester 'reality' is the structure of moral and social obligations which impose duty and responsibility, for Edmund 'reality' is self-advancement, the appetite for power and place, the ruthless assertion of individual will and, wherever necessary, the manipulation of others who may help or hinder the process. Here is the thematic link with Gonerill and Regan. Formally, in their speeches of love for Lear, they seem committed to the Lear idea of 'Nature'. But it is the brief prose exchange which closes I.1 that reveals their true commitments. They feel no love for their father, but view him with a cold and keen-eyed shrewdness calculating

**Idem*, p. 16.
†Cited *idem*, p. 39.

the best way to turn the situation to their advantage. As we have already noticed, the two sisters, and Gonerill especially, see Lear's insistence on still calling himself King, and keeping his troop of a hundred knights, as a directly *political* threat. That is their only world, as it is of their husbands (in some degree), as when we hear of the 'snuffs and packings of the Dukes' (III.1.26), the manoeuvring for position in their rivalry for complete command of the kingdom. Regan later remarks that it was a mistake to let the blinded Gloucester wander away on his own, because he would move political feelings against their rule. That is her only thought about him. Gonerill, confronted with Albany's horrified response to the news about her treatment of Lear, calls him a 'moral fool' (IV.2.58), preaching about 'humanity' when he ought to be facing the political threat to his position which Cordelia's army poses. Regan's attitude to the system of 'Nature' as a

Gonerill, Albany and Regan in V.3. (Brook's King Lear.) *(Courtesy of National Film Archive/Stills Library)*

structure of values is entirely self-serving. When Cornwall's servant attacks his master for putting out Gloucester's eye, he does so in the name of 'service' to his lord (III.7.73), implicitly invoking a 'natural' order which justifies his act. For his pains, Regan calls him 'dog', and kills him with the significant dismissal 'A *peasant* stand up thus!' (III.4.79). Similarly, we may contrast the loyalty of Kent to Lear *against* his own self-interest (as the Fool points out in II.4.69 ff.), with the loyalty of Oswald to Regan in hoping to kill the blind and helpless Gloucester as a means to self-advancement (IV.5.39–40). The instances multiply.

In contrasting the orthodox Elizabethan idea of a benignant Nature with the Hobbesian idea, Danby's point is not to make an anachronistic connection between Shakespeare and the seventeenth-century political philosopher, but to use the latter's ideas as an instance of new historical movements in Shakespeare's time, of which Hobbes's thought was a later and developed expression. We can think of Edmund as one of the Elizabethan 'new men', of the kind that worked gladly and profitably for Thomas Cromwell, authorized by Henry VIII to dispossess the Church of its lands and revenues, after his quarrel with the Pope. The traditional position, reflected in the Lear view of 'Nature', was under challenge in Shakespeare's day. Thus, James I's preoccupation with the Divine Right of Kings reflects an *insistence* upon a conception of political legitimacy—the King's authority as sanctioned by God, and at the same time involving reciprocal Christian responsibilities towards his subjects, because the idea of divine right was coming under pressure. A change in the balance of political forces was taking place: the expansionist entrepreneurial thrust of the Jacobean period; the beginnings of that conflict between King and Parliament over the issue of monopolies (that major source of political patronage whereby the King granted his supporters the right to the profitable management of certain kinds of trade) are equally marks of the early seventeenth century. *King Lear*, in that sense, Danby proposes, engages significant political and economic tensions, the more effectively for their being disguised in a legend about pre-Christian Britain.

The third term in the play's intellectual structure is provided by Cordelia. Lear's scheme of 'Nature' is self-contradictory. Edmund's view of it is, in one respect, right. To use a modern term, Lear's 'Nature' is a mystifying ideology which obscures a system of legal oppression, this being one of Lear's central discoveries in his 'madness'. Edmund 'works' this ideology to his own advantge because, in the end, it functions to legitimate power. The farcical bargaining of I.1 whereby land and revenues are calculated against love is shown for what it is: an assertion of political and familial power. But once Lear has abandoned his real power, he can no longer make the system of 'Nature' serve his needs. 'Nature' will no longer heed him, however eloquent his appeals. What he proceeds to discover is the mutuality of human *need* in the face of a natural world that owes men nothing, that far from supporting some hierarchy or social values, is neutral, indifferent, powerful both in its capacity to distress (rain, wind, barrenness), and to heal and support (the herbal medicines provided by the Doctor) according to the use that humankind makes of it. Cordelia is specifically associated with this latter sense of

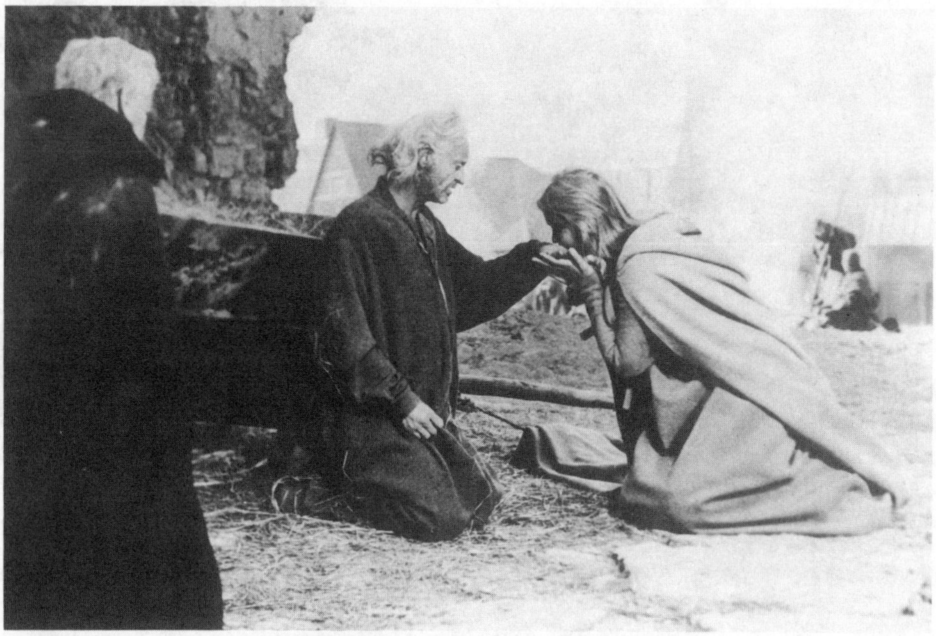

'O Look upon me, sir,/And hold your hand in benediction o'er me': Cordelia in IV.7.67–8. (*Kozintsev's* King Lear.) (*Courtesy of National Film Archive/Stills Library*)

the natural world as fructifying, and also with a quality of relationship in which the mutuality of open need is the key expression. By 'love', Cordelia means the opposite of 'power'. She opposes love to Lear's exercise of power, and only when he has thoroughly abandoned every claim to power, is he able to see what Cordelia has represented. The life he envisages with her in prison is explicitly contrasted with the continuing world of power where 'packs and sects of great ones . . . ebb and flow by the moon' (V.3.18–19). Danby links this idea with a tradition of Christian Communism, where, in Gloucester's words, 'distribution should undo excess/And each man have enough' (IV.1.69–70), represented in the medieval Lollards, in the fifteenth-century Anabaptists, and in the seventeenth-century Levellers and Diggers who were to make their presence strongly felt in the English

Civil War. It is, though, no more than a utopian vision, immediately snuffed out by the political realities, which leads Danby to see the play as a sort of Christian parable sketching the possibility of individual goodness and a just society. Its imaginative force reveals the moral emptiness of Edmund's world, leading as it does to the destruction of all its proponents in a version of the Hobbesian 'war of every man against every man', a logical result of the denial of human interdependence. Yet the fragile possibility of goodness and justice is juxtaposed with the real power of 'the corrupt world' which condemns Lear and Cordelia to 'a walled prison', and to death.*

Danby's view of the end of *King Lear*, then, though strikingly different from Bradley's, resembles it in this respect, it turns the death of Cordelia into a kind of victory. What Lear's sufferings teach us is not Bradley's implicitly Christian 'contempt of the world', but an ideal conception of relationships to be held over against this particular world. We are confronted with an opposition of absolutes. Cordelia may indeed represent all these ideal values, but in the end, what the audience see is: '*Enter Lear with Cordelia in his arms*'.

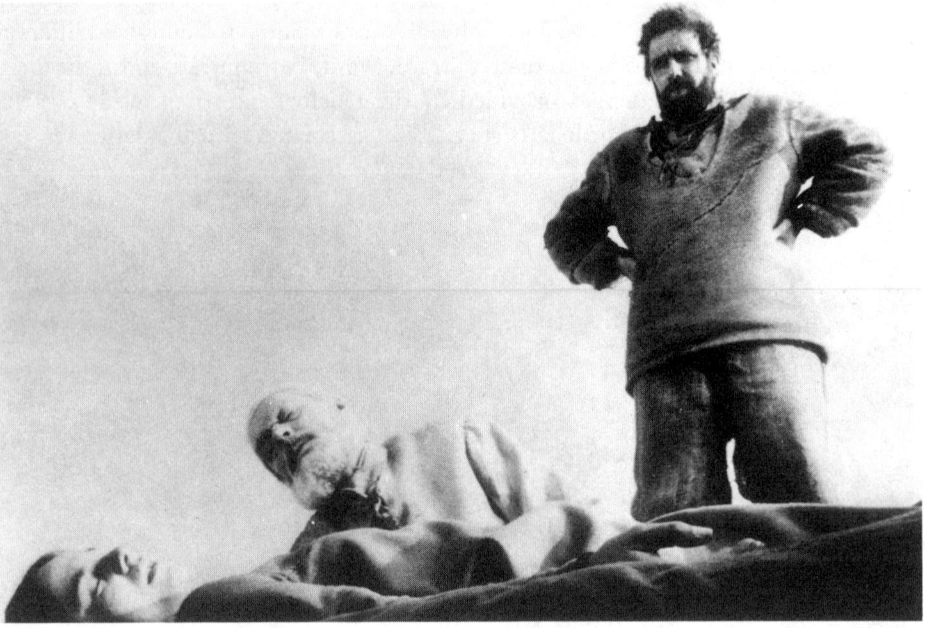

'And my poor fool is hanged!': Lear, with Kent, V.3.303. (*Brook's* King Lear.) (*Courtesy of National Film Archive/Stills Library*)

The 'suicide' of Gloucester

Let us, for the moment, leave the subject of Lear and Cordelia, and take up that of Gloucester and Edgar. Just as Lear offends against 'Nature' (as he understands the idea) so does Gloucester; and just as Cordelia suffers for her loyalty to 'Nature', and is the means of rescuing Lear, both physically and mentally, from the consequences of his offence, so Edgar rescues Gloucester. On page 16, I asked you to note not just these parallels between the two stories, but to consider what further and different issues might be raised by Gloucester's. What thoughts did you have? The nineteenth-century poet A. C. Swinburne, for example, arguing that the play was infused with a thorough-going pessimism, took Gloucester's words:

> As flies to wanton boys are we to the gods;
> They kill us for their sport.
>
> (IV.1.36–7)

*Danby, *op. cit.*, p. 195.

as expressing its deepest feeling. Would you agree? If you did, would it not also be true that such a point of view is nowhere *expressed* in the Lear story, and that its note of resignation, of human helplessness in the face of misfortune and suffering, contrasts both with Lear's passionate struggles against his fate and with Cordelia's stoical courage? And a moment before, the sight of his blinded father has prompted Edgar to say:

> O gods! Who is't can say 'I am the worst'?
> I am worse than e'er I was.
>
> And worse I may be yet. The worst is not,
> So long as we can say 'This is the worst'.

(IV.1.25–8)

Such explicit 'philosophizing' about events does seem to belong more to the Gloucester–Edgar scenes than to those involving Lear and Cordelia. Thus, as audience *we* might well recall these words of Edgar's, when we follow the events of Act V in respect of Lear and Cordelia. But Lear says nothing of the kind, as well he might have when his reunion with Cordelia is so brutally curtailed after the battle. If you take this as a clue to at least one element in the Gloucester–Edgar story, and look back again at the relevant scenes (IV.1, IV.6.1–79 and 271–86, and V.2) I think you will find further examples. In this sense, the Gloucester–Edgar scenes complement the Lear story by offering a series of reflections about human calamity, arising from what happens to Gloucester, but with suggestive general application. It is in that respect that Swinburne chose the words of Gloucester quoted above as offering a central key to Shakespeare's thinking in the play as a whole. Yet as we must constantly remind ourselves, *King Lear* is a play, not a sermon or a philosophical treatise, and considered in this light the Gloucester–Edgar scenes contribute to the theatrical experience a special characteristic.

Would you now re-read the scene of Gloucester's 'suicide', with this in mind. Is there not something about it, intrinsically 'of the theatre', which must affect our whole reading of the Gloucester story?

What actually happens in the 'suicide' scene? We learn in IV.1 that the blinded Gloucester will be guided to Dover by Edgar, still disguised as Poor Tom, to the top of 'a cliff whose high and bending head/Looks fearfully in the confinèd deep, (ll. 72–3). IV.6 opens with the two of them struggling up towards the summit of this cliff. When they reach it, there is a vivid description by Edgar of its height above the sea, a notable instance of Shakespeare's use of descriptive language to do the job for which other theatrical practices need scenery. Assured that he is standing on the edge of the cliff, Gloucester tells Edgar to leave him, and as he supposes, jumps to his death. Edgar, now pretending to be someone else at the bottom of the cliff who happens to have seen Gloucester's plunge, assures him that he had been deceived by a fiend of terrible appearance, but by a miracle, has survived his fall from the summit. Gloucester accepts both this account, and its encouraging implication that 'the clearest gods . . . have preserved' him (ll. 73–4). He resolves to bear with any further afflictions that may yet be in store. Now what does this account *omit?* I do not mean various details, but something absolutely central. It is contained in the stage direction following line 41: 'Gloucester throws himself forward'. What *actually* happens in this scene is that one character persuades another that he is on the edge of a cliff, which the audience knows is *imaginary*. Shakespeare even underlines the point in the scene's opening exchange.

> *Gloucester* When shall I come to the top of that same hill?
> *Edgar* You do climb it now. Look how we labour.
> *Gloucester* Methinks the ground is even.
> *Edgar* Horrible steep.

(IV.6.1–3)

The ground will certainly be 'even' for the audience, who see only the flat stage; just as when Gloucester makes his suicidal leap, the audience sees the *actor* playing the part fall forward onto the stage. As the Polish director and critic, Jan Kott, has said:*

> This entire scene is written for a very definite kind of theatre, namely pantomine. This pantomime only makes sense if enacted on a flat and level stage . . . The scene of the suicidal leap is also a mime. Gloucester kneels in a last prayer and then, in accordance with the tradition of the play's English performance, falls over. He is now at the bottom of the cliff. But there was no height; it was an illusion. Gloucester knelt down on an empty stage, fell over and got up.

Now, as you will recall from Professor Gurr's account of the Elizabethan public stage (Cassette 1), the pantomimic character which Kott notices in this scene really represents an intensification of a normal stage practice. Shakespeare's audience was well accustomed to the sight of actors *pretending* that such-and-such an event was happening and imaginatively cooperating with them in sustaining the momentary 'reality' of the pretence. So Gloucester's pantomime of 'suicide' is not, as a theatrical 'style' or method, quite so exceptional as Kott's comment implies. Nevertheless, there is nothing else quite like it in *King Lear*, so what does it contribute? I would suggest that it sets the event *at a certain distance from us*. Unlike, say, the blinding of Gloucester which we do not at all register as 'pantomimic', we stand a little apart from Gloucester's 'suicide'. We know it is all a pretence. Shakespeare insists that we know. And if we consider Edgar's double role, first of all as poor mad Tom bringing a blind man to the supposed edge of the cliff, pretending to go away but actually remaining on stage, then as a friendly passer-by explaining that his own previous 'appearance' was that of a hugely grotesque fiend with 'a thousand noses,/Horns whelked and waved like the enridgèd sea' (IV.6.70–1), this too sets us at a distance. Indeed, as Edgar has already said (in an explanatory nudge to those members of Shakespeare's audience who might fail to get the point) he has a distinct purpose in all this; he is subjecting Gloucester to the experience in order to cure him of his despair (IV.6.33–4). Gloucester, we may say, is being taught a lesson, and we watch him learning it; that is what the pantomime is about. That element of explicit philosophizing, of drawing general conclusions from one's experience that we have noticed in the Gloucester–Edgar scenes, here finds its own theatrical 'language' or style. That is why the pantomimic suicide concludes with Gloucester's speech saying he will despair no longer, and Edgar's confirmatory advice to 'Bear free and patient thoughts' (IV.6.79).

What now follows? Look at the text at this point; briefly remind yourself of the next episode; and consider what relationship it bears to the conclusion of the 'suicide' scene.

What follows is the scene which, in this play of scenes that again and again take the breath away with their unexpectedness and originality, can well claim to be the most astonishing of all: the mad Lear converses with the blind Gloucester. But its bearing on our immediate discussion is surely to undermine the sane 'philosophical' conclusion which Gloucester has just uttered, and which Edgar has enforced with his 'Bear free and patient thoughts'. As he goes on to say in a moment: 'I would not take this from report. It is;/And my heart breaks at it' (IV.6.142–3). *It is.* No 'philosophical' conclusion is possible in the face of what he now sees before him.

*Kott, Jan (1965) *Shakespeare our Contemporary*, Methuen, pp. 113–14.

So we have to add to the point already made about the Gloucester–Edgar scenes, that they exist in a complex interacting relationship with the Lear scenes. Their 'philosophical' conclusions are as much *tested by* what else happens in the play, as reliable generalizations about what we are to make of it. We need, as it were, to play them off against their (and Lear's) experiences rather than take them as summing up what these experiences amount to.

The critic who first grasped this fundamental point about *King Lear*, considered as a whole, was G. Wilson Knight. In his *The Wheel of Fire*—which takes its title from Lear's words to Cordelia in IV.7.47—there are two essays on *King Lear*, where Wilson Knight develops his view of the play, and to this I now want to turn. The striking aspect of Wilson Knight's argument is indicated in the title of one of the essays, '*King Lear* and The Comedy of the Grotesque'. *Comedy*? In *King Lear*? We know that the Fool jokes away at various points, but Wilson Knight's title indicates something more general.

> It may appear strange to search for any sort of comedy as a primary theme in a play whose abiding gloom is so heavy, whose reading of human destiny and human actions so starkly tragic. Yet it is an error of aesthetic judgement to regard humour as essentially trivial. Though its impact usually appears vastly different from that of tragedy, yet there is a humour that treads the brink of tears, and tragedy which needs but an infinitesimal shift of perspective to disclose the varied riches of comedy. . . . one series of facts can be treated by the artist as either comic or tragic, lending itself equivalently to both. Sometimes a great artist may achieve significant effects by a criss-cross of tears and laughter . . . A shifting flash of comedy across the pain of the purely tragic both increases the tension and suggests, vaguely, resolution and purification.*

We have, in fact, glanced at an example of this criss-cross of effects in discussing the role of the Fool (p. 19). Without in any way diminishing our feeling for Lear as he rages against the storm, the Fool sketches out the commonsense alternative—an unheroic accommodation with the realities of political power—with the effect of defining Lear's position more exactly. This is the kind of thing Wilson Knight has in view, and which he sees as central to the whole play.

Can you think of other examples? Are there incidents in the play which, by an 'infinitesimal shift of perspective' might appear comic, rather than tragic? Are there elements which lend themselves equally to comic or tragic treatment? Spend some moments on this before going on.

Surely Lear's speeches in the storm are a case in point? Do they not just fall short of the ludicrous—an old man, bellowing imprecations and denunciations against the indifferent thunder and rain? This is 'tragic' when we identify *with* Lear's feelings, but when we stand back a little . . .? Perhaps a clearer case is the 'mad trial' scene—terrible in one respect, comic in another—including Lear's parade of courteous address to his fellow-judges, one of whom is gibbering mad Tom, and Lear's fantasy that a stool is Gonerill, and so forth. Or to cite again the scene we have been considering, Gloucester's 'suicide', it would take only that slight 'shift of perspective' Wilson Knight mentions to make this comic. For is not Edgar playing a trick on Gloucester, with an effect very close to the ludicrous ('But have I fallen or no?' IV.6.56)?

It is important to remember that 'comic' as a term covers a considerable range of possibilities. The 'comedy' which Wilson Knight suggests flickers round the edges of many 'tragic' episodes in *King Lear* is the kind we call 'painful'. And the pain results from our difficulty in reconciling opposed points of view.

*Wilson Knight, G. (1949) *The Wheel of Fire*, Chatto & Windus, p. 160.

'Comedy' arises from the recognition of incongruities followed by a sense of how they might be resolved. But when this potential resolution is withheld, or felt to be out of reach, and only the *recognition* of incongruities remains, then we have the kind of 'comedy' Wilson Knight finds in *King Lear*. (If you think back to the imprisonment of Malvolio in *Twelfth Night*, you have a comparable effect approached from the 'comic' direction.) 'Comedy' moreover, prompts us to a certain detachment, or distance, from the 'comic' situation. We contemplate it, rather than participate directly in it. The simple case of the well-dressed man, hurrying to an appointment, who slips on a banana skin shows this at once: for him, it is painful and distressing; for us, as spectators who register the incongruity between human self-importance and human subjection to the laws of gravity, it is funny. And to return to Edgar's experience following his apparently successful cure for Gloucester's despair, the shift in perspective brought about by the sudden appearance of the mad Lear has the effect of an appalling joke played by fate at the expense of Edgar's well-intentioned, humane and philosophical seriousness. Edgar *experiences* the incongruous effect; we contemplate it. That is what makes it—in the sense proposed by Wilson Knight—one of those 'comic' contrasts. If you now read the rest of the scene, I think you will find that its extraordinary power derives, in part at least, from this sustained 'comic' effect, as the old King discourses, both crazily yet also with passages of lucid rationality, to the blinded Gloucester.

Wilson Knight extends his notion of an inner grotesque and awful 'comedy', finding it as central to *King Lear* as the death of Cordelia.*

> It is the last hideous joke of destiny: this—and the fact that Lear is still alive, has recovered his sanity for this.

Which might seem to bring his view of the play quite close to Swinburne's—that human suffering results from the cruel sport of the gods. But for Wilson Knight, the play as a whole differs from Gloucester's or Swinburne's conclusion because it openly *confronts* this 'ultimate cruelty of things'.

> That cruelty would be less were there not this element of comedy which I have emphasized, the insistent incongruities, which create and accompany the madness of Lear, which leap to vivid shape in the mockery of Gloucester's suicide, which are intrinsic to the texture of the whole play.

The peculiar greatness of *King Lear* resides, then, in the searching and fearless way in which it presents this truth about life. Wilson Knight goes on to add to this account of the play, pointing to some more affirmative qualities (Edgar's loyalty, Cordelia's love), noting also Lear's resemblance to Job in his stubborn preoccupation with the issue of Justice. But here his argument is not unlike that of some Christian views of the play. The distinctive character of his essay is, I think, best represented in the point about 'comedy'. And it is, I suggest, interesting that it connects so directly with the theatrical conventions within which the play was conceived, as the discussion on pages 51–2 indicates. The play sets forth fictional events which we *watch*, as well as directly feel. Gloucester's 'suicide' in that respect, too, may be thought to illustrate the texture of the play as a whole.

'Black' readings of King Lear

Let us conclude this survey of some overviews of *King Lear* by considering readings of the play, which refuse the consolatory implications of Christian, or proto-Christian, interpretations. Such readings point to aspects of our own

*Wilson Knight, *op. cit.*, p. 174.

century, for, as the editor remarks, 'It seems to have been some time during the Second World War that [*King Lear*] replaced *Hamlet* in popular esteem' (set text, p. 7).

We have already mentioned the Polish critic Jan Kott. The chapter in his influential book, *Shakespeare our Contemporary*, from which we have already briefly quoted, is called '*King Lear* and *Endgame*', and the allusion to Samuel Beckett's play of that name highlights Kott's general approach. Beckett's plays are in his estimation, peculiarly works of our time, and Shakespeare's contemporary relevance can best be brought out by noting what both playwrights have in common. His discussion of *King Lear* thus contains almost as many illustrations from Beckett's plays, as from Shakespeare's tragedy. Kott's account of the Gloucester 'suicide' scene stresses, as we have seen, its pantomimic theatrical method, which has its roots in contemporary Elizabethan stage practice. But his reasons for drawing attention to it reflect his conviction that Shakespeare is 'our contemporary', that is to say, *Beckettian.* Pantomime, he argues is the art of the clown whose mimic postures on an empty stage are an analogy for the contemporary human situation. In our time:*

> established values have been overthrown, and there is no appeal to God, Nature, or History, from the tortures inflicted by the cruel world, the clown becomes the central figure in the theatre. He accompanies the exiled trio—the King, the nobleman and his son—on their cruel wanderings through the endless night which has fallen on the world; through the 'cold night' which in Shakespeare's *King Lear*, 'will turn us all to fools and madmen'.

Gloucester's 'suicide' is 'clownish' in this way, a piece of tragic buffoonery. For Kott, tragedy in *King Lear* is expressed through such 'clowning' as is more extensively illustrated in the Lear–Gloucester scene which follows. In a universe with neither gods—and we have seen that the gods in *King Lear*, however invoked have no effective influence—nor a humane moral order, the human passion for 'meaningfulness' can only be endlessly frustrated; and moreover, frustrated in a cruel and mocking fashion. This is the world which *King Lear* presents:†

> The theme of *King Lear* is the decay and fall of the world. The play opens like the Histories, with the division of the realm and the king's abdication. It also ends like the Histories, with the proclamation of a new king. Between the prologue and the epilogue there is a civil war. But unlike the Histories and Tragedies, in *King Lear* the world is not healed again . . . In the epilogues to the Histories and Tragedies the new monarch invites those present to his coronation. In *King Lear* there will be no coronation. There is no one whom Edgar can invite to it. Everybody has died or been murdered. Gloucester was right when he said: 'This great world/Shall so wear out to naught'. Those who have survived—Edgar, Albany and Kent—are, as Lear has been, just 'ruin'd pieces of nature'.

That Kott is highlighting a very important element in *King Lear*, it is easy to agree. Like Wilson Knight, he wants us to face the grotesque and cruel features of the *King Lear* universe, and he refuses any suggestion that the play 'justifies' them. He invites us to confirm that the moral disorder, against which good, if also faulty, men like Gloucester and Lear in their different ways uselessly pit themselves reflects the deepest truths about our own time. You might want to object that despite the historical catastrophes of our century—past, continuing, perhaps still to come—Kott's view is partial. Yet, there still would be, would there not, a case

*Kott, *op. cit.*, p. 112.
†*Idem*, pp. 120–1.

to answer? These are issues too complex to debate here, and in any case, individual readers will respond to Kott's general view of our time according to their own beliefs. But what *can* be explored, within the more limited context of our discussion of *King Lear*, is whether Kott overstates his case.

What is your view of this? Does his account (which I have had to state very briefly) reflect the spirit of the play, as a whole, or is it selective? In thinking about this, you might find it useful to look again at the group of quotations listed in page 27 of this block, and recall—or indeed review—your own decision about which best represented the play.

What Kott omits, it seems to me, is adequate recognition of the distinct presence in the play of positive moral qualities, unambiguous in certain of the characters (Kent, Cordelia, Edgar) and in cloudier form in some others (Gloucester's declaration of loyalty to Lear, Albany's words about Gonerill). It is true that these moral affirmations are not, at the level of power, *successful.* Kott is surely right to insist that the play as a whole shows the destruction, or absence, of a moral order, sustained and sustainable. But that is not the same as an entire absence of admirable moral qualities. His account of the play's conclusion, too, seems over-emphatic. How did you respond to it? Are the survivors 'ruin'd pieces of Nature'? We sense exhaustion, certainly, and are not exactly surprised. What other mood would be right than 'general woe' (V.3.317)? Kent has had enough, and doesn't want to live any longer. And Edgar's closing sentences show that, as the character who has personally suffered a lot, and, worse, been the witness of his father's suffering, he has something of the measure of the experiences the play sets before us. Yet he remains undestroyed. Perhaps the most interesting thing about his closing speech is that he has stopped trying to draw explicit conclusions. 'Ripeness is all' (V.2.11) he had said to his father. He has now perhaps learned what 'ripeness' amounts to. But that doesn't mean that he is now a 'ruin'd piece of Nature', surely? I am not arguing here for a 'positive' conclusion for *King Lear* to set against Kott's 'negative' one, but rather to suggest that the text is far less emphatic than Kott's reading. A third objection to Kott's account would be that the morally wicked characters, in the pursuit of their self-interested schemes, succeed only in destroying themselves. Cornwall dies at the hand of a despised servant; Gonerill and Regan compete for Edmund, who responds entirely according to the 'Nature' he has openly expounded; one sister poisons the other, then commits suicide; Edmund is killed by his brother. That we do not read these events as (in Johnson's words) the triumph of 'natural justice', is not a reason for forgetting them.

The other reading that I want to mention is by Barbara Everett, entitled 'The New *King Lear*', originally appearing in *The Critical Quarterly*, but conveniently available in the collection of essays on the play, edited by Frank Kermode, in the Macmillan Casebook Series.* Everett's principal target is the conception of *King Lear* as a complex moral allegory of the kind that Bradley develops (see above pages 42–4), or more generally of the Christian readings we have glanced at, in which Lear struggles painfully through a series of terrible experiences which collectively teach him profound spiritual truths. While not a 'black' reading in the manner of Kott, Everett's account equally rejects the consolatory version of *King Lear* that, so to speak, shows the sufferings of the good characters to be *worthwhile.* This, she argues, is to abstract an intellectual pattern from the play, which fails to take into account the power of its poetic and dramatic rendering of experience.

*Everett, Barbara (1960 'The New *King Lear*', *The Critical Quarterly*, vol. 2, no. iv, pp. 325–39; reprinted in Kermode (1969) *King Lear: A Selection of Critical Essays*, Macmillan.

> . . . the chief reason, then, why one feels doubt about an extremely allegorical interpretation of the play is not that such an interpretation can be said to be 'wrong', but simply that the play succeeds so well in another way. Rather than setting up an absolute dichotomy between the 'world' and the 'soul' . . . it shows a continual relation between the two that strengthens and enriches both; so that a sense of extreme evil can be conveyed in a phrase of casual malice—('What need one?' 'And all night, too.')—and a sense of extreme good in the commonest expressions of a woman's kindness. (See Cordelia's speech in IV.7.30–42.)†

Everett goes on to suggest that:

> . . . the forms of suffering in the play are transformed not so much by being seen *sub specie aeternatis*, but rather by being seen as forms of intense life. If the play exhilarates, it is less because 'Cordelia, from the time of Tate, has always retired with victory and felicity', whether temporal or spiritual, than because it exhibits a poetic power in the writing of the play itself, in the consciousness given to its central character, and in the responsive awareness of audience and reader, that can understand and endure imaginatively actions of great suffering, and by understanding, master them.§

As audience or reader, that is, provided we respond fully to the play's language, we receive not just representations of pain and suffering, but 'transformations' of them. It is the intensity and power of Lear's response to his plight that we should concentrate on; an intensity shared in varying degrees by the wicked characters as well as the good ones, and closely bound in with the expressive power of the writing. Where would you turn for illustrations of Everett's argument here? There are, of course, all the big speeches—some included in the Performance Cassette 6(p)—Lear's curses, his raging at the storm, his prayer of compassion for the 'poor naked wretches', his exchanges with Gloucester in IV.6, the reunion with Cordelia; or there are Edgar's wonderful accounts of the cliff near Dover, or Cordelia's own few speeches in Act IV. But perhaps Everett's point is also well illustrated in some equally memorable briefer quotations. My own choice here would be:

> Why should a dog, a horse, a rat have life,
> And thou no breath at all? Thou'lt come no more;
> Never, never, never, never, never.
> Pray you undo this button. Thank you, sir.
>
> (V.3.304–7)

With such writing, one is reminded of T. S. Eliot's idea that the best poetry speaks 'beyond poetry', its language no longer 'poetic'.

Would you now re-read the second quotation from Everett's essay? She uses a term for the play's overall effect that I wonder if you noticed, and perhaps found surprising?

The phrase and term is in the fourth line of the quotation 'the play *exhilarates*'. This is, surely, a remarkable description for the play's effect. Everett's argument here is not that the play in any sense finally *cheers you up*. It is precisely that kind of moral–allegorical account that she wishes to contest. She asserts rather that the exhilaration derives from the play's brilliant powers of expression which assert a

†Kermode, *op. cit.*, p. 201.
§*Idem*, pp. 201–2.

human *mastery* of the dreadful experiences it puts before us. The implication seems to be that the creative affirmation rendered by means of Shakespeare's language represents the final answer to the worst that life can deal out. If a thing can be uttered, then one is no longer subject to it.

In reading these different accounts of the play, you may have begun to ask whether we were moving towards some conclusive interpretation? But complex masterpieces are, in this respect, disobliging. They are not puzzles which patience, skill and amassed learning will ultimately solve. Matthew Arnold wrote a poem about Shakespeare beginning:

> Others abide our question. Thou art free.
> We ask and ask. Thou smilest and art still.

Such apostrophes to authors are not in the modern style, but perhaps may have a bearing on their works. *King Lear* does not smile, yet we might think of it as remaining 'still', at the centre of the swirl of overlapping and conflicting views which devoted critics have elaborated about it. As Frank Kermode remarks in the introduction to his anthology of essays, the play is 'patient of many interpretations'.* Interpretation, moreover, is collaborative, and what we get out of *King Lear* will depend on what we bring to it. The preceding discussion has aimed to distinguish some important assumptions which different critics have brought to the task of reading it, and in that way, may help to clarify your own.

GM

The Language of the Play

Edgar: diction and narrative structure

For the subject of detailed work on Shakespeare's language in this block I have chosen Edgar, and I want to look at all his appearances in the play in the order in which they occur. Yet in doing so, I shall not ask you to think of *King Lear* as a sequential narrative, but as a pattern of carefully juxtaposed fragments, more like a film montage than a traditional story. It's often been suggested that if Shakespeare were alive today he would be a film director, and though fanciful, the idea is illuminating. A lot of the *story* of *King Lear* seems to have been left on the cutting-room floor. The narrative consists not of a fluid continuum, but of a succession of carefully juxtaposed sequences that is far from naturalistic.

To begin, reread I.1.1–32; I.2 and II.1, where you will find plenty you might want to say about Gloucester and his bastard son Edmund. But what is there to say about Edgar? And if not much, why is this so?

Unless his betrayal had taken place off stage altogether (which it might have done) Edgar could hardly have been given fewer words to say. In contrast both Edmund and his father are in their different ways verbose. This has actually led some people to feel that they 'prefer' the self-confident villainy of Edmund to his brother's apparent colourlessness. Why doesn't Edgar stand up for himself, they ask, and decide that such a 'wet' deserves what he gets. This is about as far from the point as protesting that Cordelia might have been more tactful and saved a lot of trouble. You can put together a certain amount of information about Edgar. He is a year older than Edmund, was lawfully conceived—and perhaps his nature is, accordingly, less sportful (I.1.8–23 and I.2.11–14). If you really wanted to rake

*Kermode, *op. cit.*, p. 13.

the text for cues in order to give Edgar a positive identity you could take Edmund's hint at I.2.14 and make Edgar one of the 'whole tribe of fops'—but that hardly squares with Edmund's ironic emphasis on Edgar's legitimacy (I.2.18–21) with all its connotations of dullness.

It's not just because Edmund is prejudiced that this method is inappropriate. But it's exactly the technique I suggested *was* appropriate for determining the presentation of characters in *Twelfth Night*. Here as always you have to balance close study against the long view. And what would be the point of trying to construct an elaborate Edgar here where his part is so minimal—and will change so soon? Edgar only enters after Edmund's plot has, to all intents, already succeeded. And the manner of his entrance suggests something automatic and predictable (see I.2.132). Edmund's 'sigh like Tom o'Bedlam' is ironic, for after one more brief appearance and half a dozen words (II.1.32) Edgar flees from his father's pursuit to assume the status of just such a crazy beggar. So, his first appearances do hardly more than establish him as the object of his brother's malice and his father's over-hasty credulity.

Read II.3. What is the function of this speech, and in particular the significance of the last phrase: 'Edgar I nothing am'?

Edgar, you might say, he nothing was. In the great Russian director Kozintsev's film of this play we see Edgar escape the pursuit of his father's agents, and take hiding amongst some desolate rocks from where he sees a troop of Bedlam beggars making their way through the beginning of the winter's storms towards the hovel where Lear will later find shelter amongst the homeless and the afflicted. It is a fine interpretation in cinematic terms of what Shakespeare had to achieve by quite different means.

It's easy to forget (because we don't see it happen) that Gloucester does not merely abandon his legitimate son.

> Let him fly far,
> Not in this land shall he remain uncaught;
> And found—dispatch.
>
> (II.1.55–7)

'All ports I'll bar' he declares later in the same scene (l. 79), and sure enough Edgar finds the whole country patrolled against him (II.3.1–5). It's an element to be remembered when one comes across references to the 'weakness' of Gloucester. What Kozintsev could show, Shakespeare has to make Edgar describe. This is not speech that claims to be the expression of a character's inner experience.

So how would you define its qualities? It may help you to look very carefully at its position in the structure of the whole play.

It gives us a certain amount of information necessary to the plot: that Edgar has been pursued and that he intends to disguise himself. But its main purpose is surely to tell us about the suffering of the poor and helpless. It is a kind of transition, an introduction to the searing and changing experience of the storm into which the very next scene precipitates Lear, his Fool, Kent—and Edgar's father. Perhaps it is unnecessary. Perhaps it is undramatic. After all, so much of what this speech merely states will be actively discovered in the succeeding scenes: compare Edgar's

> . . . the basest and most poorest shape
> That ever penury, in contempt of man,
> Brought near to beast . . .
>
> (II.3.7–9)

with Lear at III.4.28–32 and 99–105.

Yet surely it is too powerful, too compassionate, too moving for us to feel it is redundant. And when we consider the central episodes of the play as a whole perhaps we are also impressed by the *sanity* of this. Passionate and horrifying though it is, nevertheless this is discourse in which the presence of securely rational thought is palpable. There is nothing that is impressionistic or naturalistic about this passage. You may want to go on from there and claim that the speech is there to assure us that despite the disguise and the manner Edgar will shortly assume, he is not really mad at all. But I want to make two objections. First, in the storm scenes themselves the text does very little to remind us that this naked beggar may be as sane as you or I. And, secondly, to argue thus is to be still seeing the part in terms of personality, where the fragments are expected to form a coherent whole that will somehow seem like a man. Think of the whole of Edgar's story for a moment. Given that, is it really feasible to expect him to be presented in realist terms?

I don't deny that the speech has a practical function in terms of the plot. Edgar was too much of a cipher in his previous appearances for it to be sensible to expect an audience to recognize him had he merely turned up as Poor Tom. Without this speech it would have been necessary to introduce some very disruptive 'asides' into III.4. But its major function seems to me to be choric: a highly articulate equivalent of the first warning grumbles of thunder that are heard towards the end of the next scene.

You cannot consider Edgar's part in the storm scenes in isolation, so would you now re-read III.2, III.4 and III.6. I always want to call Edgar 'Poor Tom' during these scenes. Is there any reason why I shouldn't? Is there indeed any reason why Shakespeare did not simply introduce a 'real' beggar here, if one was needed, rather than a nobleman's son in disguise?

Disguise figures prominently in *Twelfth Night* and *Measure for Measure*, and Hamlet's 'madness' can be seen as a kind of disguise too. But in all those instances we are constantly aware of the 'real' identity of the disguised person. Here, it is not until late in the sequence (III.6.59) that Edgar unambiguously reminds us of who he 'really' is. Perhaps that is because he has so thoroughly *been* Poor Tom.

It is difficult enough to keep pace with the wisdom in folly of the Fool's enigmatic speeches. Poor Tom's gibberish seems even more impenetrable at first.

His function in these scenes is complex. Stripped to the skin, he is the living symbol of the compassionate understanding that Lear begins to achieve:

> Thou art the thing itself! Unaccommodated man is no more but such a poor, bare, forked animal as thou art.
>
> (III.4.103–4)

He is even perhaps the exemplar that leads Lear to this wisdom: he goes before the King in madness, and shows him the way. You may object that Edgar isn't really mad. But both the physical and the linguistic transformation are so complete that the question of whether Edgar remains in touch with his rational self throughout these scenes becomes unimportant. We see and hear Poor Tom—and he is mad.

If you consult the notes on Tom's speeches you may think you are expected to be able to decode, or make sense of them; but really it is obvious that Shakespeare intended their sense to be thickly veiled. Consider the problems that Shakespeare had imposed upon himself with the decision to present two mutually reflecting plots. Edgar, in his own person once again, sums up the parallels at the end of the sequence: 'He childed as I fathered' (III.6.108).

During the storm, Lear struggles with the injustices he has suffered from his daughters. Simultaneously Edgar as Tom endures the full brunt of the suffering that his father's injustice has imposed upon him. It would be tedious, mechanical and ridiculous for the two characters to work out their rage in the same language. And to Lear, whose arrival at this crisis has been traced so scrupulously, belongs the greater degree of articulation here. In comparison, what drove Edgar to the heath has been only sketched. All detail has been excluded. And so, correspondingly, the language of Edgar's purgatorial experience here is more impressionistic, less detailed. It is a broad wash of painful sound, from which meaningful details only emerge spasmodically, to be half understood.

But if we look at Edgar's language here in more detail, we can see that there is some kind of form to its apparent formlessness.

Look at the passage from Gloucester's entrance at III.4.110 to the end of that scene.

The Fool's phrase 'a walking fire' seems an ironic description of mild-mannered Gloucester. But to his son he has been a merciless pursuer. And Edgar spits and snarls at him like a cornered animal. The hideous notion of demonic possession underlines the whole scene. Gloucester is the devil ('foul fiend Flibbertigibbet'), a creature of darkness, the cause of deformities and diseases that mar nature; he 'hunts the poor creature of earth'. And Gloucester, his eyes still intact, sees and does not recognize, hears and does not understand, that Poor Tom, who

> . . . in the fury of his heart, when the foul fiend rages, eats cow-dung for sallets, swallows the old rat and the ditch-dog, drinks the green mantle of the standing pool . . .
>
> (III.4.124–7)

is his outcast son. That Gloucester sees Tom (and does not see him) is made clear by his well-bred distress that Lear should have 'no better company' (III.4.135). Whereon Tom bitterly comments, 'The prince of darkness is a gentleman'. And when Gloucester sanctimoniously observes, 'Our flesh and blood, my lord, is grown so vile/That it doth hate what gets it' his own wronged flesh and blood cries out 'Poor Tom's a-cold'. Cordelia never reproaches her father for his injustice.

Edgar's speeches are characterized by a number of recurrent motifs. Predominant is the idea of pursuit by the devil under many names over a cold and harsh landscape.

> Through the sharp hawthorn blow the winds.
>
> (III.4.45)

> . . . Poor Tom . . . whom the foul fiend hath led through fire and through flame, through ford and whirlpool, o'er bog and quagmire . . .
>
> (III.4.49–51)

The names of animals abound. Look through and see how many you can find. The whole play is well studded with references to animals, but they come particularly thick and fast here, from one who is—as he himself (at II.3.9) and Lear both recognize—close to the state of a beast. In Kozintsev's film, which used only a fraction of Shakespeare's text, much of what was omitted from the verbal dimension was transmitted into the visual element. Dogs of all kinds, horses, birds of prey and the carcasses of hunted animals gave to the film a note of savagery which in Shakespeare's text is located in its figurative language. And it may help us to see the function of Edgar's language in relation to Lear's if we think of it as a kind of background that only intermittently sharpens into focus. It isn't a language that *we* can 'read' clearly; but that does not mean it is not powerfully expressive.

But Lear apparently can 'read' Edgar. Notice how both Kent and the Fool try to step in between the King and Poor Tom (III.4.63–109). But Lear will not be deflected. He has much to learn from Tom, whom he calls 'learnèd Theban', 'Noble philosopher' and 'my philosopher' (III.4.150, 165 and 170). Edith Sitwell suggested that 'learnèd Theban' is a reference to Oedipus, who solved the riddle of the sphinx. The answer is 'Man', and it is in Poor Tom that Lear discovers what Man really is. Well, perhaps. My point is not so much to decode the obscurities here as suggest that when probed, what may look at first like gibberish can turn out to fit in with a consistent, though blurred, whole.

At one point however the blur does seem consistent. Look at Tom's answer to Lear's question 'What hast thou been?' (III.4.81). At first it seems as though this might be a realistic account of what Edgar might indeed have been—though, as we have seen, before he became Poor Tom the play gave Edgar only the thinnest kind of identity. Then (at line 87) the clauses begin to rush again, and the sense thickens and curdles into nonsense.

I suggested that in II.3 Edgar was allocated the introduction to the storm sequence. At the end of III.6 he is given its concluding speech. What do you notice about the language here?

The succession of pat rhymes is rather a shock. After what has gone before it seems jaunty, almost trivial. The sane man has re-emerged from the experience of Poor Tom, but surely his observations are almost unbearably trite. Words like 'free things', 'happy shows', 'o'erskip', 'mates', 'fellowship' and 'light' reinforce this impression. They seem to have been lightly chosen. Some commentators have thought the passage spurious, but I think it is possible to see it as part of Shakespeare's overall design, in which Edgar only gradually accumulates the wisdom of experience.

In contrast, the speech that introduces Edgar's next part in the story (IV.1.1–9) is deliberative and sonorous.

Re-read IV.I now.

If you were seeing or reading the play for the first time, and were familiar with the conventions of Renaissance drama, speeches such as this and II.3 (as well as the storm scenes) would have told you that Shakespeare is building Edgar's part into something far more significant than his minimal early appearances might have seemed to promise. In modern productions this speech often follows the interval.

The diction of this speech is much more impersonal than that which ended III.6. It is not until line 7 that Edgar relates the general propositions that he is asserting to his own predicament. If you look carefully at the construction of the six preceding lines you can see that their construction avoids any use of personal pronouns because it is not himself, or Lear, that he is really talking about. He is proposing a general moral law, in which human identity, subject to Fortune, is reduced to no more than a 'thing' (l. 3).

Compare

> How light and portable my pain seems now,
> When that which makes me bend makes the King bow
>
> (III.6.106–7)

with

> The lamentable change is from the best;
> The worst returns to laughter.
>
> (IV.1.5–6)

There's a huge distance between the trite observations of the first to the considered, abstract language of the second. As Graham Martin has suggested already (pp. 24–7), several characters make the kind of general statement about their experience which sounds like a summary of the play's 'message'. But it never is. Here Edgar's confident generalization about human suffering is immediately shattered by the appearance of his newly-blinded father.

> O gods! Who is't can say 'I am at the worst'?
> I am worse than e'er I was . . .
> And worse I may be yet. The worst is not,
> So long as we can say 'This is the worst'.
>
> (IV.1.25–8)

But notice how the despair of the first pair of lines is succeeded by the courageous acceptance of the second. Notice too how simple these lines are: unadorned monosyllables in plain order in which the repeated word 'worst' sounds like a muffled drum.

We noticed that in the storm sequence Edgar's 'real' identity was almost forgotten until the end. But here, forced in even more terrible circumstances to assume Poor Tom again, the difference between the man and his disguise is emphatic. Shakespeare stresses the pain it causes Edgar to shift into Tom's speech once more: 'Poor Tom's a cold. (*Aside*) I cannot daub it further./. . . And yet I must' (IV.1.51–3) I do not think we are ever supposed to feel that Poor Tom is an *easy* imitation of madness, and through the confusion of Edgar's speech in the crazed idiom once again we can glimpse a suggestion that as Tom, Edgar is *possessed*: 'Five fiends have been in Poor Tom at once'. But notice too that the father whom in that idiom he formerly cursed, he now blesses.

Now re-read carefully IV.6 and identify, according to the variations in his diction, the number of distinct parts that Edgar plays.

You will have noticed that as soon as Edgar and Gloucester's location has been identified, Shakespeare draws attention to the change in Edgar.

> Methinks thy voice is altered, and thou speak'st
> In better phrase and matter than thou didst.
>
> (IV.6.7–8)

Poor Tom's voice has gone—though the horror of that role is recalled later in the scene when Edgar, in yet another identity, claims to have seen from beneath the non-existent cliff a creature whose eyes

> Were two full moons; he had a thousand noses,
> Horns whelked and waved like the enridgèd sea.
> It was some fiend.
>
> (IV.6.69–72)

Edgar's changes of role and function during this scene are so numerous that I think we are less conscious of an Edgar than of a fluid, infinitely responsive presence.

But do you agree? Should the actor charged with this role attempt to establish a continuous Edgar, or fully *be* all the distinct parts that Edgar plays?

In II.3 we saw that Edgar was less a character than a descriptive function. Here too his first function is to describe—but not this time the 'reality' of the Bedlam beggar. It is frequently pointed out that since Shakespeare was writing for an almost bare stage, his characters have to express the scenery. Here that conventional function becomes bizarre, for the cliff which Edgar creates in words is not there. And yet he acknowledged that the fiction may be as effective as Dover cliff itself:

> And yet I know not how conceit may rob
> The treasury of life, when life itself
> Yields to the theft. Had he been where he thought,
> By this had thought been past . . .
>
> (IV.6.42–5)

Notice once again how the complex figurative rhetoric of the first two and a half lines here is succeeded by the concrete simplicity that follows, in which the contrast between 'thought' as verb and 'thought' as noun renders so economically the full horror of Edgar's device.

Gloucester's 'fall' is a very difficult moment to stage. To succeed, it must partly depend on the strength of the illusion that Edgar's description creates, so it is worth looking at how the speech is put together. The description is contained—almost wrapped—in two invocations of vertigo, and the successive items in the description mimic fall. Each is more distant than the last: the birds, 'that wing the midway air', the samphire gatherer *hanging* half way down, the fishermen on the beach, the boat, the sea itself. The inner eye travels towards the indistinct—

> . . . The murmuring surge
> That on th'unnumbered idle pebble chafes
> Cannot be heard so high . . .
>
> (IV.6.20–2)

And each thing that can be 'seen' appears smaller than it is: the birds no more than beetles, the samphire gatherer no larger than his own head and so on. Distance obliterates the proper dimensions of each.

This imaginary cliff also marks the location of a metaphoric cliff: a crisis for Gloucester—and for Edgar. We saw how Gloucester's betrayal of his son was merely sketched in. So too is the present change in Edgar from Poor Tom to his father's guardian.

> Why I do trifle thus with his despair
> Is done to cure it.
>
> (IV.6.33–4)

It simply happens. And the new persona who greets Gloucester at the bottom of the cliff, so to speak, is a man of certain moral authority.

> . . . Therefore, thou happy father,
> Think that the clearest gods, who make them honours
> Of men's impossibilities, have preserved thee . . .
> Bear free and patient thoughts.
>
> (IV.6.72–80)

And Gloucester, chastened, responds meekly. The son has become his father's father.

In the dialogue with the crazy Lear which follows, Edgar is hardly more than an onlooker, and his few interjections only register the pain of what he sees. He is there only as a witness, but in such a role—and we remember that he was a witness in the storm too—he has become one who 'by the art of known and feeling sorrows' has become 'pregnant to good pity' (IV.6.222–3). He is also allocated a practical function. Through his brief dialogue with the Gentleman who comes in pursuit of Lear, we learn that Cordelia is near. And when he kills Oswald, Gonerill's creature, we are made aware that all the characters are massing for the final confrontation.

But why do you think Edgar shifts into a rustic accent for the encounter with Oswald?

I don't really know. Certainly to disguise himself from Oswald and to make his voice suit his appearance. Neither Gloucester nor Lear (one blind, the other mad) would notice any discrepancy. But such a practical explanation is too boring to be satisfactory. Edgar has been a great variety of social roles, and this rude peasant is another of them. The killing of Oswald is distasteful ('I am only sorry he had no other deathsman'—notice the poised idiom here) and maybe the new voice is a kind of suggestion that it is not 'really' Edgar who is soiled by the deed. It's also possible that Shakespeare wants to echo the first retaliatory death in the play, when a 'peasant' (III.7.79) kills Cornwall as he goes to put out Gloucester's second eye. Whatever the intention, the effect is an Edgar who is still amorphous.

And there is still one change left to come in the scene. If you look back to the earlier parts you will see that Edgar addresses Gloucester and later the Gentleman as his social superiors. He frequently calls both 'sir' and when he calls Gloucester 'father' it is partly as a younger man addressing an older and respected one. In these roles he is a decent, articulate and straightforward man of the middling sort with an innate dignity that gives authority to his moral prescriptions. But now the discovery of the letter Oswald was carrying impels Edgar back into his legally inherited social role. And the polished locutions of the courtier begin to slide into his language:

> Leave, gentle wax; and manners blame us not;
> To know our enemies' minds we rip their hearts;
> Their papers is more lawful. (IV.6.259–61)

This conjunction of the polite with the savage is like Hamlet—and so is his final speech in the scene. It is vigorous and well-studded with educated words. Edgar is about to take the place in the action that his birth demands. He is himself again. Or what he never was.

The fight between Edgar and Edmund, V.3. (Brook's King Lear.) *(Courtesy of National Film Archive/Stills Library)*

'thou art a traitor,/False to thy gods, thy brother, and thy father', *V.3.131–2.* (*Brook's* King Lear.) (*Courtesy of National Film Archive/ Stills Library*)

Edgar's next appearance (at V.1.38) is once again in disguise. It is not as himself, or as a man of anything like his own social position that Edgar brings Albany Gonerill's letter to Edmund. But what exactly he pretends to be is mysterious. He is 'a man so poor' and yet he can command Albany's trumpets; 'wretched', he can nevertheless 'produce a champion'. He is like a figure in Arthurian romance who comes unheralded to announce the impending arrival of some unknown knight in the lists.

Shakespeare left himself too much to do in the fifth act, and Edgar's next appearance (in V.2) is a clumsy contrivance in which he reports the news of Cordelia's defeat and (in the manner of 'Bear free and patient thoughts' at IV.6.80) hastily bucks up his still disconsolate father. But that over, a more measured pace is re-established and maintained throughout the crowded final scene.

Albany, obeying the disguised Edgar's instructions, has his trumpets sound to summon the 'champion' who will challenge Edmund in single combat. The whole episode is consciously 'stagey': 'An interlude!' as Gonerill contemptuously exclaims (V.3.90). Albany, in the traditional manner, throws down his gauntlet, and Edmund his. A challenge is formally proclaimed. The trumpet sounds twice. And sure enough the unknown knight appears.

> Know, my name is lost,
> By treason's tooth bare-gnawn and canker-bit:
> Yet am I noble as the adversary
> I come to cope.
>
> (V.3.119–22)

It is possible to mistake the tone here for fairy-tale. But for an Elizabethan and Jacobean audiences the Arthurian romances, in which such encounters frequently occur, were a possible vehicle of the highest moral truths. The greatest example was Edmund Spencer's graceful and profound allegory, *The Faerie Queene*. To stress the romance elements in this duel is to raise a sordid intrigue to a higher moral plane. And Edgar's announcement that his 'name is lost' is not merely a formal convention, a piece of pantomime in keeping with this kind of tournament. His name, his position, his very nature have indeed been lost: remember 'Edgar I nothing am' in II.3. The speech at lines 125–39 is, as you will recognize, another new voice.

Study it now and try to define some of its characteristic qualities.

This is the language of chivalry, of a knightly code already archaic in the early seventeenth century but still respected as the expression of a lofty ideal. It is a highly artificial posture, and the very idea that the right of Edgar's cause can be proved by the strength of his arm has to be set against the cruelly realistic death of Cordelia. In Edgar, virtue triumphs. But Cordelia's goodness cannot save her.

Edgar's speech is measured, stately, even leisurely: like the formal poses fencers assume even before a mortal contest. (Think of the end of *Hamlet*.) He doesn't simply call Edmund 'a most toad-spotted traitor' and leap upon him. Words like 'privilege', 'honours', 'oath' and 'profession' announce that it is as a man dedicated to an ideal of virtuous conduct that Edgar fights, and not solely to redress his personal injuries. The word 'maugre' was already archaic: these are the values of another time. The speech is packed with careful lists:

> . . . I protest
> Maugre thy strength, place, youth, and eminence,
> Despite thy victor sword and fire-new fortune,
> Thy valour and thy heart, thou art a traitor,
> False to thy gods, thy brother, and thy father . . .
>
> (V.3.128–32)

And Edmund responds in the same idiom.

What is the purpose of this elaborate charade? Simply to enliven a last act in which most of the other deaths take place off-stage with an impressive set-piece duel? Perhaps, but surely it also enhances Edgar, and confirms the value of his part in the story. We are immediately reminded of just how much of the play he has witnessed in the dialogue with Albany that follows. He calls his sufferings a 'pilgrimage' (l. 196)—a penitential journey in search of grace. A man who was negligible, even nothing, an unstable, unconfirmed identity, emerges here as the strongest surviving voice. Albany, technically the victor, is never so clear. Edgar now is the authorative expressor of both the plays' sternest justice

> The dark and vicious place where thee he got
> Cost him his eyes.
>
> (V.3.170–1)

and its most poignant compassion:

> . . . O, our life's sweetness,
> That we the pain of death would hourly die
> Rather than die at once . . .
>
> (V.3.182–4)

And yet his moral achievement is futile. Even if a little of his goodness rubs off on Edmund, it is too late to save Cordelia. This is not the place to give a full discussion to the play's ending, but I do want to consider why it is that Edgar is usually apportioned the final speech.

This is traditionally allocated to the highest-ranking survivor. Hence in *Hamlet* it goes to Fortinbras, and by the same rule here it should go to Albany—indeed, in the Quarto text it does. But he, I have suggested, remains shadowy—a very 'bitty' part that never quite firms up. More important, he has seen less of the play than Edgar, who has, uniquely, been a witness to Lear's as well as his father's suffering. Hamlet, you'll remember, tells Horatio

> Absent thee from felicity awhile,
> And in this harsh world draw thy breath in pain
> To tell my story . . .
>
> (*Hamlet*, V.2.345–7)

and Edgar is the only one who can tell *this* story—indeed, this aspect of his function has already been realized when he tells it to Albany. He is not merely a survivor, he is the vessel into whom so much of the play's wisdom and suffering has been poured. He is perhaps the representative within the play of its audience—without whom the story would be wasted indeed.

What I have attempted to show is how Edgar is *made*. The part is an accumulation of fragments, and of many varieties of idiom. It is, I think, an extreme, even a unique case, but nevertheless one which should challenge some of our too-easily maintained notions about Shakespeare's character and his dramatic techniques. For we can never imagine that Shakespeare began by thinking of what kind of man Edgar is. Neither personality nor type is the spring from which this particular aspect of the creation flows, for Edgar is neither. Shakespeare's naturalism, his 'truth to life' is so moving, so beguiling, that it is all too easy to see the imitation of life and nature as the fundamental principle of his art.

If you scrutinize the plot of the play in order to search for some precise relation between cause and effect, or how characters 'know' about the movements of others, or how the time sequence works, it is revealed to be incoherent in this respect. At that level it is not realistic at all. But such inconsistencies are easily swallowed or ignored, and we console ourselves with the naturalism of the emotions expressed. Yet as we have seen over and over again as soon as we look closely at this expression we see how small is the part that realistic imitation plays. We have repeatedly asked of all the texts in the course: what kind of play is this? We also need to ask: what kind of a thing is a play?

To such questions the answer must be either brief or very, very long. My brief answer is that it is an idea, displayed by its division and distribution into named parts. These named parts need not be human at all. In the Block II Interval I referred to the medieval morality plays, in which many of the parts take the name of abstract qualities. And though in Shakespeare's plays few of the parts are other than human, their abstract and symbolic qualities are palpable—especially in *King Lear*. It is to these parts or divisions of the idea that the whole responsibility of narrative and exposition is allocated. There is no independent authorial presence to fill in the story or corroborate the significance of the characters' actions—as there is in the classic 'realist' novel, for example. Nor can more than a tiny proportion of the expression of the play's ideas ever be assigned to scenery or inanimate, unspeaking objects as in film. In Shakespeare's plays there is so very little that is not verbal: a kiss, a fight, a gift bestowed, a death. Speech is virtually the plays' sole dimension—and not simply speech, but for the preponderant part, *dialogue*. Is naturalism the only standard to be applied to such a massive artifice? Is the story of your life a succession of dialogues? For sure, it might be expressed as such, but in the process of expression lies the transmutation of the idea or the experience into Shakespeare's kind of drama.

Almost everything that is not speech is left out. Or to put it more positively, the totality of experience is rendered as speech. A simple example is the use of speech for scene-setting. I've also referred to the functions of figurative language, which again are not a common property of 'real' speech. The proportion of speech to silence in Shakespeare's plays—where, indeed, speech is almost continuous, was vividly revealed by Olivier's films of some of the plays—and by any mere film recording of a stage production. One convention reveals another: in films people simply don't talk so much.

If we tell a story, we don't usually render it entirely in direct speech. Shakespeare does. But the story is only part of the play. Not, I think, a small part, though one that is largely determined and even limited by the dialogue mode.

Shakespeare inevitably concentrates his narration on those moments when things happen during or because of speech. It's rather absurd to talk about things that happen off-stage, because in what possible sense do they happen at all? Sometimes, for the sake of continuity, a character will fill in the narrative—and frequently at such moments the pace lags. And sometimes, as we have seen, the necessary connections were so far from coming into existence at all that Shakespeare simply did not bother with them.

But the plays are not just stories. To say that they express ideas can suggest that Shakespeare might have done better as a politician or a philosopher. But in these plays ideas are not subject to the full constraints of logic nor of doctrine. The artist is under no obligation to make ideas add up as if they were mathematical qualities. The unruly principle does not have to be wrestled into submission, nor the exception made to prove the rule. Consider the etymological connections between the words *dialogue* and *dialectic*. In both, the Greek prefix '*dia*' means *through* or *thoroughly* or *apart* or *across*. Hence *dialogue* means something more like *words crossing*, and *dialectic* the testing of truth through discussion. It is in this sense that Shakespeare's plays are dialectic. As you'll remember, Professor John Danby described *Antony and Cleopatra* as a 'dialectic'. In that play issues divide fairly neatly into two opposing sides.

But ideas, qualities, principles and so on are not drawn up in only two opposing ranks in *King Lear*. Nor are they in *Measure for Measure*. Both these plays consist of a debate that proceeds from a multiplicity of points of view, and to a remarkable degree each one is given its due, unprejudiced by authorial favour. It is even possible to allow that Gonerill and Regan have their rights.

But what a part like Edgar's exemplifies is that although all the disparate aspects of the dialectic are located in speech they are not apportioned solely in terms of character. It is not as simple as two, three or four different people embodying the same number of different points of view which are then set out in a debate amongst them. There is a level at which the dialectic of the play is extra-personal. Edgar's part is an amalgam of separate fragments, each with its distinct idiom, and created for a variety of functions within the play. It could have been divided amongst several minor characters, not units under one name. The wronged child, mirror-image of the wronged father, is only part of his role. We can see why, in the eighteenth century, Nahum Tate, who found the play's ending intolerable, should have rewritten it to end with a marriage between Edgar and Cordelia. It was not just a wish for a more optimistic conclusion. Their parts are already dovetailed. both begin from 'nothing'. There is no equivalent in Edgar's story of the reconciliation between the wronged child and the hasty-judging parent. But there is in Cordelia's. Forgiveness flows from the plot in which it is dramatically achieved to suffuse the other in which it is only minimally reported. On the other hand, Edgar's exposure to the central experiences of madness, pain and degradation make it dramatically unnecessary for Cordelia to appear in the middle of the play. Despite the parallelism of the two plots, there is no redundant repetition in this play. Its values and their antitheses are transferable, not restricted to the individual. The play's incontrovertible evil is philosophically expounded in Edmund, shown in action in Gonerill and Regan. Its good is learned through Edgar's experience, acted by Cordelia. 'A tear is an intellectual thing', said William Blake, and though *King Lear* may move us to the profoundest emotion, we should not forget to pay tribute to the extraordinarily detached and controlled intelligence by which it was constructed.

Postscript: a second opinion

Your editor's most detailed account of Edgar appears on pages 35–7 of the set text, and in many respects it is very different from mine. You should read the whole introduction, but for further passages which challenge, sometimes corroborate and sometimes contradict mine, especially look at the top paragraph on page 11, pages 12, 14, 15, 22 and 24–7.

CPH

Forum

King Lear*: the text and the director*

Under this title I wish to consider a few key moments in the play, and to discuss their stage interpretation. Critics rightly invite interpreters of the play, whether as readers or as actors, always to go back to the text, though they acknowledge that three and a half centuries of critical and interpretative discussion have failed to produce anything like unanimity of opinion about a single play of Shakespeare's. One unavoidable aspect of critical discussion concerns the text itself, and the difficulty, perhaps even the impossibility, of establishing a definitive one. As you know from Cassette 2, the textual problem varies from play to play; and the detailed interpretation of different texts, and their relation to one another, is the job of an editor. Following that editorial process, any director of a Shakespeare play has first to determine his own text, not only to tailor the play to the length acceptable in the theatre concerned, but to do so in ways which reinforce his line of interpretation. The latter criterion may strike you at first as a kind of sophisticated cheating, because any selection from a text seems to imply bias, as well as to query the dramaturgic skill of the playwright. One check is to follow the practice of John Barton, one of the RSC's directors: conduct rehearsals with the Folio text open at the right place. From time to time a theatre company offers a performance of a 'complete text', using the Folio, or, if a play has a particularly interesting Quarto text, as *Hamlet* does, that. (It would be the Second Quarto of *Hamlet*, not the first.)

My first point for discussion is a weighty one, which involves textual exactness and possibly textual adjustment in decisions about the interpretation which might be offered. It concerns a moment in the play when the director and leading actor have to make a big theatrical statement, at IV.6.80. It is the point at which the two suffering old men are brought together for the first time, thus uniting main plot and sub-plot, which remain interwoven from now until the end of the play. Lear has reappeared about half an hour (if anything like a full text is played) after being carried off the stage in exhausted sleep at III.6.99.

Remind yourself of the placing of the scene and its main events: then decide whether the 'madness' of Lear is different from that of III.6, and suggest what implications, if any, there might be in that prolonged absence from the stage of the tragic hero.

First, we must review the extraordinary accumulation of detail in the build-up to this scene. In brief:

(1) 'Dover' has been on almost everyone's lips for many scenes now; the *place* of the tragic denouement, which has been offered as one of hope, is a point of convergence for Cordelia and her forces, the English army with its good and bad components, and the two ancient outcasts, Lear and Gloucester.

(2) In the interim of Lear's absence, the purgatorial suffering of Gloucester has brought him to a comparable stage: he is blind, and has been brought by Edgar past the point of wishing to end his life. In this as in other matters, the sub-plot is more explicit than the main one, and its clear formulations throw light on the more mysterious processes of the Lear plot:

. . . Henceforth I'll bear
Affliction till it do cry out itself
'Enough, enough', and die . . .

(IV.6.75–7)

(3) Since Lear's previous appearance, the hope represented by Cordelia has been filled out. In II.2 she was represented only by a letter to Kent; in III.1 Kent sends to her by the Gentleman, and in IV.3 the same Gentleman describes her compassion and good intentions towards Lear. In IV.4 we at last see her again, for the first time since I.1; there, besides expressing her intention to rescue her father, she gives the commands of a competent general. (IV.3 appears in the Quarto, but was excluded from the Folio, in my view because the beautiful emblematic description of Cordelia by the Gentleman does not advance the action, which continues only when Cordelia appears in the next scene.)
(4) During Lear's absence, the long-threatened division between Albany and Cornwall (mentioned by Curan in II.1) has turned into another kind of opposition: a sexual contest between Gonerill and Regan for the favours of Edmund, which involves, on Gonerill's side, the assassination of Albany, the surviving Duke and husband. In the scene under consideration now, IV.6, the killing of Oswald and the discovery on his body of Gonerill's letter to Edmund effectively foreshadow a main part of the ending of the play, especially when taken together with the outburst of Albany against tyranny and cruelty in IV.2—another character who has long been absent from the stage, this time since I.4. Until IV.2 the audience would assume that the camps of both dukes would be equally interested in the deaths of Lear and Gloucester, because of the known position of Gonerill and Regan.

Now to the core of the matter: the long absence of Lear from the stage, and the changed nature of his behaviour when he returns in IV.6. First, a note on Shakespeare's construction of tragedies in which the heroes' parts are both central and long. In every mature tragedy except *Othello* (in which the longest part is that of Iago, not Othello), at about three-fifths of the way through the play Shakespeare leaves the tragic hero off-stage while he develops the counter-action (in the case of *King Lear* including the sub-plot) to the point at which the final round of the action may begin. Like Hamlet, Macbeth and Coriolanus, Lear is off stage for between four and five hundred lines. One theory of theatre people is that this fourth act 'rest' is needed by the leading actor to recharge his batteries for his assault on the ending of the play. But the effort of acting the first three-fifths of the play has been such that, although the actor playing the hero resumes refreshed in a minor sense, and hence different in his disposition, his tiredness is reflected in a kind of tension which goes well with the tragic climax to be enacted. That tension is generated by his will to project the essence of his part by means of almost exhausted physical resources of voice, body and spirit. I have actually seen a TV director keep his leading actress on the studio floor when she was crying out for a rest, with the calculated intention of getting a more raw and shattering performance out of her. It worked, though only by means of the strong support given by the other actor in a tremendous duologue.

Hamlet's half-accepting fatalism after his return from sea to Denmark, Macbeth's profound despair and defiance of fear at the approach of the English forces to Dunsinane, and Coriolanus's desperate last-act attempts to resolve the contradiction between desire for revenge on Rome and obedient devotion to his mother, all seem to me likely to be played more convincingly if the actor is in the state I have suggested. But how does such an argument apply to the playing of Lear from IV.6.80 onwards?

In this interim between his first and second collapses from exhaustion (the first is in III.6, the second before the start of IV.7, and the third and last at the end of the play), Lear seems to me to be in a state of settled madness, devoid of self-pity and full of outgoing sympathy for all humankind. It is the one scene of which it could be said that in it Lear becomes a sort of king of humanity. Only then is he free of considerations of self—though, when captured by Cordelia's soldiers he objectively sees his fate as worthy of tears:

> Why, this would make a man a man of salt,
> To use his eyes for garden water-pots,
> Ay, and laying autumn's dust . . .
>
> (IV.6.196–8)

The curiously carefree mood of Lear at the start of the scene in which he moralizes crazedly about his life was represented in Michael Elliott's 1982 TV production, with Olivier as Lear, in the following way. After Edgar's 'Bear free and patient thoughts,' which was spoken to the newly resolute Gloucester, as the text directs, the rest of Edgar's short speech acknowledging the arrival of Lear was cut, and the camera moved to shots of Lear washing his smalls in a stream, and then gutting a snared rabbit and eating its chitterlings raw. Edgar and Gloucester approached Lear only after a live mouse had been fed with imaginary cheese, and were at once invited to 'give the word'.

What effect do you think was intended, and how do you rate its success?

I can see the intention. It is to show Lear, by visual means and an adjustment to the text, as happily independent (though crazed) and in harmony with nature. (You might note that this is the only point in the play when either of the aged sufferers is not attended by a comforter-guardian.) So this ploy establishes the 'new' Lear immediately he appears, instead of allowing him to reveal himself progressively through his just clear-sightedness and compassion as the scene unfolds: qualities which appear the greater because Lear remains preoccupied with ingratitude:

> . . . for Gloucester's bastard son
> Was kinder to his father than my daughters
> Got 'tween the lawful sheets.
>
> (ll. 114–6)

and with his disillusionment about love: 'No, do thy worst, blind Cupid; I'll not love' (l. 138). You might well think it pure indulgence to introduce 'low' matters like the washing of smalls and the preparation of food into such a titanic play, which is otherwise free of anything else of the kind. But the facilities of television do tempt a director to use resources the stage has difficulty in offering.

Another detail about the 'new' Lear is affected by the text the director accepts or adjusts. The stage direction at Lear's entry is, in the Folio, 'Enter Lear', and in the Quarto, 'Enter Lear mad'. Many modern editors, including yours, accept the sentimental suggestion of the eighteenth-century editor Capell: 'Enter Lear fantastically dressed with wild flowers'. I must say I prefer to follow Alexander (William Shakespeare: *The Complete Works*, London and Glasgow, 1951): 'Enter Lear fantastically dressed with weeds', because that is how Cordelia described him at the beginning of IV.4. Weeds symbolize his state of mind, flowers don't.

None of my other examples involves textual problems or modification. My first is taken from the first scene, which G. K. Hunter discusses on pages 27–33 of his introduction to the set text.

The question I pose is one of acting interpretation: how would you as director wish the actresses playing Gonerill and Regan, as well as the rest of the company on stage, to perform lines 55–76? Again, before answering, re-read the text, and think about the context as well as about what happens.

Two broad interpretations suggest themselves to me. The first, which admits of variations, is that the two sisters speak spontaneously in harmony with their characters as progressively revealed through the play. That is to say, their chosen language—as Shakespearean characters who naturally 'speak poetry' which contains imagery suitable to the speaker—shows 'their concern for the metallic and legalistic aspects of the exchange, statements traded for land, or rather (more abstractly) power' (Hunter, p. 32). I think Hunter is right, and remains right about the sisters' speech even if my second broad interpretation is accepted.

This is that the speeches of both women are performances which have been carefully prepared. Not rehearsed in detailed phrasing, because this would mean that rivalry between the two could not exist, as it clearly does; but 'carefully prepared' because in the second speech of the play Gloucester talks to Kent as if the coming division of the kingdom were common knowledge. The scene in which the three daughters are asked to express their love for their father, and to accept commensurate rewards of land, is therefore a ritual, the conditions of which are known in advance. Lear's smooth and predetermined apportionment of a defined part of his kingdom to Gonerill (ll. 63 ff.) and automatic passing on to Regan ('What says our second daughter?') confirm the lack of tension inherent in the formality. Now, the performance of a ritual recognized as such from within the play is different from the performance of any other kind of stage action. If it is to be understood by the theatre audience as a ritual, then the principals in the action as well as the audience on stage must positively convey such an import. If that is right, Gonerill and Regan must speak as if trying to work out or perhaps recall practised extravagances of compliment, and the on-stage audience—suitors and courtiers—must dutifully reward each speaker in turn for her performance with murmurs of approbation, which might be capped by applause at the conclusion. The subsequent refusal of Cordelia to accept the ritual—though she truly expresses her love for her father when pressed—then has a psychologically and textually exact climactic brilliance. And the fault of Lear—self-indulgent paranoia, delusive expression of god-like kingship, call it what you will—which sets the whole tragic sequence in motion is correctly focussed.

With regard to this scene, few critics seem to have appreciated that in the setting up of his ritual, with its favourable outcome for Cordelia, Lear has prepared a massive public snub for his two elder daughters:

> . . . what can you say to draw
> A third more *opulent* than your sisters'? Speak!
>
> (ll. 85–6)

You might ask, how could this textual truth be emphasized in performance? I think my plan would be to make Lear listen almost negligently to Gonerill's and Regan's protestations, and busy himself with the map, or perhaps with smiling at Cordelia.

The third question I wish to pose concerns the acting part of Gonerill alone. How does she respond to the curse of her father at I.4.272–86? Re-read the passage and consider its context in the light of your knowledge of the whole play, before trying to answer.

Gielgud, in his 1949 Stratford production, which is remembered as containing his finest performance of Lear, and Adrian Noble in the 1982–3 RSC production, both represented Gonerill's reaction to Lear's cursing of her womb as one of horror and violent physical molestation. So you will understand that this interpretation is not unusual. But do you agree with it? If you look at the calculated cruelty and self-possession of Gonerill's two previous speeches ('This admiration . . .' and 'You strike my people . . .'), you may wonder why a woman whose father has just called her 'degenerate bastard' should worry at having her womb cursed with sterility by the same speaker, even if it is in the presence of her husband. Gonerill's response is to regard Lear's outburst with cold distaste, as the raving of a powerless dotard, as her reply to Albany, whom she at once and casually squashes, indicates:

> Never afflict yourself to know more of it;
> But let his disposition have that scope
> As dotage gives it.
>
> (I.4.288–90)

One might note, in discussing this, that the prospect of a woman outraged in her deepest being, as in the version I dismiss, always makes good theatre sensation.

I add a production note to the above. It concerns the justice of Gonerill's case against Lear. Some directors follow Lear's sympathies in the matter and bring on Lear and his men at I.4.7 in the spirit of

> My train are men of choice and rarest parts,
> That all particulars of duty know
>
> (I.4.260–1)

While others follow Gonerill's view that Lear's retinue

> Do hourly carp and quarrel, breaking forth
> In rank and not-to-be-endured riots . . .
>
> (I.4.198–9)

A look at Lear's entry, with the Folio stage direction and Lear's first speech, convinces me that Lear and company should erupt on this scene like a riot:

> *Hornes within. Enter Lear and Attendants*
>
> *Lear* Let me not stay a jot for dinner, go get it ready.

If any of Gonerill's terms are still not believed, it is worth looking at 'Not only, sir, this your all-licensed fool . . .' (l. 196). We have evidence of both sisters' hatred of the free-speaking clown: when I was working on a production of *King Lear*, the man who was playing the Fool was so impressed by it that at Regan's famous 'What need one?' (II.4.258), he said at rehearsal, from his cowering position at Lear's side, 'I suppose that one's me?' Formally and textually, Regan is referring to knights, but they are not present, and in this production a brilliant *aperçu* of stage dynamics was in fact adopted by us: Regan pointed at the Fool, who was terrified.

My fourth question is about weeping. Here are five references to tears, one made by Cordelia, one by Edgar, and three by Lear. Can you use them to suggest whether Shakespeare has any system of values in mind—that is, whether tears stand for anything except, conventionally, sorrow?

(1) *Cordelia* The jewels of our father, with washed eyes
Cordelia leaves you . . .

(I.1.268–9)

(2) *Lear* . . . —Old fond eyes,
Beweep this cause again, I'll pluck ye out
And cast you with the waters that you loose
To temper clay . . .

(I.4.298–301)

(3) *Edgar* (*aside*) My tears begin to take his part so much
They mar my counterfeiting.

(III.6.59–60)

(4) *Lear* If thou wilt weep my fortunes, take my eyes.

(IV.6.177)

(5) *Lear* Thou art a soul in bliss; but I am bound
Upon a wheel of fire, that mine own tears
Do scald like molten lead.

(IV.7.46–8)

At first sight, just from these five quotations, which are selected from many possible ones, two main sorts of tears seem to be defined: those which are wept in vexatious self-pity (Lear, in the second quotation, is remembering with shame the tears he shed at Gonerill's first cruel opposition (I.4.295)), and those which show grief at the plight of others. But we must look particularly at examples (1) and (5). If in connection with (1) you looked up Hunter's note to ascertain the meaning of 'washed', you found two conflicting meanings; if you went to the Arden *King Lear* (ed. Kenneth Muir), you found only Hunter's first meaning, 'washed with tears'. To my mind that is wholly inappropriate: the last thing Cordelia would do on parting with her viperous sisters would be to weep, as her 'I know you what you are' clearly proclaims. She is choosing that her eyes be washed clean of tears as a value judgement on the occasion, and only a sentimental director would require tears of the actress at this point. In Michael Elliott's TV production, to which I have already referred, the actress is required to weep at her father's brusque dismissal (I.1.262–5), and turns to Gonerill and Regan with eyes still wet; which takes the force out of Cordelia's judgement on her sisters. In example (5), Lear's tears do relate to himself, but not in vexatious self-pity. On the contrary, these are purgatorial tears shed as part of his redemptive process: they show his 'sovereign shame' (IV.3.42) at the memory of the great wrong he did Cordelia. The tears of Edgar at the sight of the enfeebled Lear imagining his own hounds turning upon him (3) are straightforward tokens of compassion, like Cordelia's tears when she and Lear appear as Edmund's captives ('Wipe thine eyes'—V.3.23). This little exercise could be extended to a discussion of every other reference to tears, with no different result. Shakespeare's use of tears is always precise, an item in the emotional and moral structures of the play, and never merely a conventional sign of sorrow.

My last directorial puzzle is: what dramatic effects are required when Edmund appears after the English victory with Lear and Cordelia as prisoners (V.3.1–26)?

This is a short scene of such unbearable tension and pathos that close analysis is not often directed at it. I propose to make two points, to link them together, and leave the ideas with you to ponder. The first point I owe to Bertram Joseph, who discusses in his edition of the play (University of London Press, 1966) some notable ironies, including this one. The scene starts with Edmund's order to the soldiers to take away Lear and Cordelia; but they do not move. Nor do they eighteen lines later, when Edmund repeats his order in the same words. (Exact repetitions usually require extra emphasis, do they not?) The soldiers never take them away; they go of their own accord, at Lear's suggestion. Professor Joseph's point is that only Albany, the titular commander of the soldiers (though Gonerill and Regan both seek to dispute it), could give an order affecting royal prisoners which the soldiers would obey. The second point is that Cordelia wishes to stay to 'see these daughters and these sisters', and if she had prevailed in that wish, instead of complying with Lear's desire to be alone with her in prison, both their lives would have been saved, because Albany, who enters only a few moments later, is intent on preserving them with all honour. Some students with whom I have discussed this find it a weakness in Cordelia, who has previously shown up well as a military commander (IV.4.22–3), that she gives way to Lear here. Perhaps she should have been thinking of her husband and the half of her love which belonged to him, instead of full-heartedly and tearfully following her doting father who, in spiritual *extremis* of bliss over the reunion, can think only of being caged like a singing bird with his beloved daughter? If this interpretation is followed, the stage actions must show (a) that Lear's bliss is fatuous in political and military terms, (b) that Cordelia's practical judgement has deserted her, and (c) that the soldiers—apart from the Captain who offers to do the 'man's work' of killing a dotard and a princess—will not take the order Edmund gives them. Perhaps the NCO under the Captain could prevent by a gesture the movement of soldiers to carry out the orders of their superior?

Upon these thoughts, I leave you thinking about the responsibilities of a director of *King Lear*.

BS

Part Three
Tragedy

Introduction

IN Part Two, we considered a number of views of *King Lear*, partly for their intrinsic interest, but partly also as a way of prompting you to look at the text as a whole, first from one angle, then from another, considering the arguments for and against each particular view.

In this section, I want to open up a more general question, though one with immediate application to *King Lear*, as also to *Hamlet* and *Antony and Cleopatra*, the question of 'tragedy' as a genre. What is 'tragedy'? And why do we enjoy it (if indeed 'enjoy' is the word)? As with all such questions of definition, we need to remember that a word signifies, not a thing, but a concept, that concepts are often, certainly in this case, complex, and derive some of their meaning from a relationship with other concepts. 'Tragedy' is thus partly defined by a relationship of contrast with 'comedy', and vice versa. Moreover, we need to beware of supposing that there is some 'essence of tragedy' present in varying quantities in certain plays, which careful analysis can discover. This is clear when we remember that 'tragedy' has been differently conceived within different historical and cultural situations.

Here, for example, are four such definitions, two of which you may recognize from Cicely Havely's survey of the context of Shakespearean drama (Block II, pp. 89–91). Read them over, then briefly describe how they differ. (It will be enough here to pick out one major point about each definition, not present in the others.)

(1) Aristotle, *The Poetics*, *c.* 330 BC*

> A tragedy, then, is the imitation of an action that is serious and also, as having magnitude, complete in itself; in language with pleasurable accessories, each kind brought in separately in parts of the work; in a dramatic, not in a narrative form; with incidents arousing pity and fear, wherewith to accomplish its catharsis of such emotions.

(2) Chaucer, *The Canterbury Tales*, *c.* 1390†

> Tragedie is to seyn a certeyn storie,
> As olde bookes maken us memorie,
> Of hym that stood in greet prosperitee,
> And is yfallen out of heigh degree,
> Into myserie, and endeth wretchedly.

(3) Sir Philip Sidney, *An Apology for Poetry*, 1595§

> . . . the high and excellent Tragedy, that openeth the greatest wounds, and showeth forth the ulcers that are covered with tissue; that maketh kings fear to be tyrants, and tyrants manifest their tyrannical humours; that, with stirring the affects of admiration and commiseration, teacheth the uncertainty of this world, and upon how weak foundations gilden roofs are builded.

*Bywater, Ingram (ed.) (1920) *Aristotle's 'The Poetics'*, Oxford, p. 35.
†Robinson, F. M. (ed.) (1957) *The Works of Geoffrey Chaucer*, OUP, p. 199.
§In Smith, C. Gregory (ed.) (1934) *Elizabethan Critical Essays*, OUP, vol. 1, p. 177.

(4) Raymond Williams, *Modern Tragedy*, 1966¶

> . . . the three characteristically new systems of thinking, in our own time—Marxism, Freudianism, Existentialism—are all, in their most common form, tragic. Man can achieve his full life only after violent conflict; man is essentially frustrated, and divided against himself, while he lives in society; man is torn by intolerable contradictions, in a condition of essential absurdity. From these ordinary propositions, and from their combination in so many single minds, it is not surprising that so much tragedy has in fact emerged.

Briefly, how do these differ? Aristotle says that tragedy is a '*dramatic*, not a narrative form'; Chaucer mentions narrative alone ('a certeyn *storie*'); Sidney conceives tragedy as having direct moral influence ('maketh kings fear to be tyrants', etc.); while Williams sees tragedy as emerging from 'systems of thinking ... Marxism, Freudianism, Existentialism', in other words, as a review of life, rather than a particular dramatic or literary form. So, if in your general reading, you come across the phrase 'the tradition of tragedy', you should be immediately sceptical. Such 'traditions' are characteristically, and silently, selective. There *are* overlappings and resemblances between the tragedies produced within different cultures, or within one culture at different times, but the differences are equally important. Thus, Sidney influenced by Aristotle, agrees that tragedy has a particular psychological effect but their accounts differ: Aristotle speaks of a 'catharsis' (i.e. purging) of the emotions of pity and fear, Sidney merely of '*stirring* affects of admiration and commiseration'. Chaucer's definition implies an element of moral teaching, but far more emphatic and pointed than Sidney's. While the idea of a 'tragic view of life', present in Williams' account, only begins to make its appearance in post-1800 discussions of the genre. This extension of meaning may be familiar to you in the idea, for example, that the novels of Thomas Hardy, or the poetry of W. B. Yeats, communicate 'a tragic philosophy of life'.

Renaissance tragedy

What ideas about 'tragedy' were current in Shakespeare's time? We have already touched on one such idea on page 37 above. Tragedies, by representing 'The Fall of Princes', proved the instability of human achievements, and in the above quotation from Sidney's *Apology*, you will notice the same conception. Yet Sidney's account raises again the difficulty we touched on in discussing the kind of play *Measure for Measure* was (Block V, pp. 57–65). Contemporary Elizabethan theorizing about 'tragedy' as about 'comedy', drew its ideas from Greek and Roman drama. Renaissance Humanism maintained that the pre-Christian cultures of Greece and Rome should provide the models and ideals for contemporary writing in the vernacular culture, so that this, though not composed in the classical languages, might nevertheless be worthy of comparison with the classical achievement. Such influences encouraged the composition, and in some degree the performance, of an 'academic' kind of contemporary play, and it is these that Sidney has in mind, not the native product from such as Kyd, Marlow or Shakespeare, none of whose plays in any case he could have known, for he died in 1586. Sidney's words can be seen to strike this 'academic' note in its notion of the performance of actual tragedies to a kingly audience. For as one critic has remarked, the whole idea is 'slightly comical, if we think of a row of stalls full of kings being shown what happens to tyrants'.* Sidney's distance from the actual

¶Williams, Raymond (1966) *Modern Tragedy*, Chatto & Windus, p. 189.
*Rossiter, A. P. (1961) *Angel with Horns*, Longman, pp. 258–9.

dramatic production of the Elizabethan stage is further brought out by this comment:*

> All theyr Playes be neither right Tragedies, nor right Comedies; mingling Kings and Clownes, not because the matter so carrieth it, but thrust in Clownes by head and shoulders, to play a part in maiesticall matters, with neither decencie nor discretion: So as neither the admiration and commiseration, nor the right sportfulness, is by their mungrell Tragy-comedie obtained.

The thrusting in of 'Clownes by head and shoulders, to play a part in maiesticall matters' immediately calls to mind the role of the Fool in *King Lear*, which Sidney could not have approved. Here again he is advancing a classical idea. 'Tragedy' should deal in a stately manner with noble personages and lofty themes in a consistently solemn mood. 'Tragicomedy' was a mixed 'kind', both socially because it included other than noble persons, and in tone, because the comic elements offended against the appropriate 'tragic' manner, much as rock music would be thought to outrage the general tone of Wagner's *The Ring*. Perhaps *Hamlet*, in 'showing forth the ulcers' in the state of Denmark might have met with Sidney's approval, but the biting comedy arising from the Prince's 'madness' would certainly have worried him. A play he doubtless would have approved is Jonson's *Sejanus His Fall* (1603), for in 'tragedy' as well as in 'comedy', Jonson struggled to realize classical ideas in the public theatres. Unsullied by any breath of the 'comic', this play dramatized the rise and fall of Sejanus, the ambitious confidant and chief minister of the Roman Emperor Tiberius. Such a tale would have political meanings for—or at least, about—the high courtiers of James I, busily advancing their schemes for power and position, and perhaps even carry a veiled warning to the monarch about the danger of encouraging his favourite courtiers too far. (If so, we have to add that James ignored the message.) But you will have read enough of Shakespeare to know how little his plays 'teach' the simple direct moral lesson that Sidney has in mind. We may think that his remark about 'stirring the affects of admiration and commiseration' (i.e. wonder and sympathy) reflects the complexity of our response to Shakespeare's tragic heroes and heroines. But notice again what Sidney thinks the result should be! To teach:

> the uncertainty of this world, and upon how weak foundations gilden roofs are builded.

We have seen that this moral met with the approval of Sir Walter Ralegh (a powerful courtier fallen on evil days), and it has its roots both in the medieval idea about the value of 'tragedie', and in some classical writings. But so stated, what relevance has it to Shakespeare's tragic plays? As Arnold Kettle has already pointed out (Block II, pp. 7–10), *Antony and Cleopatra* is a tragedy-with-a-difference, so if Sidney's formula fails to apply there, we needn't be surprised. But do *Hamlet* or *King Lear* teach lessons about 'the uncertainty of this world'? My answer would be: *Hamlet* not at all, and *King Lear* only in such a way as to underline how very limited Sidney's idea is.

What has to be faced then is that such ideas about 'tragedy' do not help us with Shakespeare's work, because it was so much the product of the native dramatic practice, very little influenced by classical models. It is precisely this lack of application of Renaissance (or subsequent neo-classical) theorizing about 'tragedy' to the vernacular Elizabethan–Jacobean product that has been one powerful stimulus to further debates about the nature of tragic art, to which we can now turn.

*In Smith, *op. cit.*, p. 199.

Hegel and Bradley

German thinkers and critics of the Romantic period played a very important part in establishing Shakespeare's subsequent, and indeed present, reputation. During the eighteenth century, the prestige of the Greek and Roman classics, and even more of those Renaissance and later commentators who elaborated what came to be known as neo-classical criticism, meant that Shakespeare's work, though greatly admired, was felt to fall short of the highest achievement. Johnson, for example, no slavish follower of neo-classicism, nevertheless preferred Shakespeare's comedies to his tragedies, on the grounds that the language of the latter was insufficiently 'decorous', failing to maintain the note of solemn eloquence absolutely necessary to tragedy—as conceived by neo-classical critics. English critics of the Romantic period—Coleridge, Hazlitt, Lamb—broke away from neo-classical assumptions to write with originality and penetration about Shakespeare's poetry and plays but they had been anticipated by German critics, for whom Shakespeare became a sort of culture-hero, assisting them in their own struggle against neo-classicism. Of these, the most systematic and influential was the philosopher G. W. F. Hegel (1770–1831), who included brilliant analyses of many Shakespeare plays in his writings on literature, drama and aesthetics. Hegel elaborated a general view of 'tragedy', mainly based on Greek drama, but that also applied to the plays of his own day, and to some Shakespearean examples. Here is a paragraph expressing one central idea.*

> The *tragic* destruction of figures whose ethical life is on the highest plane can interest and elevate us and reconcile us to its occurrence only in so far as they come on the scene in opposition to one another together with equally justified but different ethical powers which have come into collision through misfortune . . . Out of this situation there arises the right and wrong of both parties and therefore the true ethical Idea, which, purified and in triumph over this one-sidedness is thereby reconciled in *us*. Accordingly, it is not the highest in us which perishes; we are elevated not by the destruction of the best but by the triumph of the true.

Hegel is not easy reading, but I hope you will have seen the force of his main point here. He is tackling, in a general way, an issue which all tragedies present us with: the destruction of something valuable and good. Why do we contemplate this with any other feelings than protest and sorrow? Why do we—in some sense—enjoy it? Or if 'enjoy' is too positive a term, why do we assent to it? Hegel distinguishes between our response to ordinary human suffering (which we ought to act directly to cure or alleviate), and to the fictional suffering represented in tragedies. We contemplate this, not less sympathetically, but with greater detachment, an attitude brought about by the fact that tragic conflict arises from the collision of 'two equally justified but different ethical powers'. Tragedies present us not with conflicts between good and evil, but between one partial good and another. The pain we experience at the destruction of one or other or both of these 'goods' or 'ethical powers' leads to the affirmation of a more complex sense of ethical justice which incorporates the limited rightness of each protagonist. Hence, as the extract concludes, 'we are elevated not by the destruction of the best, but by the *triumph of the true*' (my italics). Hegel draws his ideal examples of such drama from the work of Sophocles and Aeschylus, but his analysis evidently offers some purchase on *Antony and Cleopatra*. Here, we contemplate a conflict between 'Roman' virtues represented in Octavius Caesar and 'Egyptian' virtues represented in Cleopatra, with Antony torn between them and eventually choosing 'Egypt'. The catastrophe, then, shows the destruction of 'Egyptian' by 'Roman' qualities, yet

*In Paolucci, A. and H. (eds.) (1975) *Hegel on Tragedy*, Harper & Row, p. 237.

leaves us, not with a one-sided victory by the latter, so much as a powerful impression of the limitations of both 'ethical powers'. Though we may wonder whether Hegel's 'triumph of the true' is also an effect of the play's ending, such an analysis is certainly more illuminating than the Renaissance idea of a moral warning to those in high places. Indeed, such complexity of attitude towards the catastrophes in tragic drama is surely always present. We lament Hamlet's death (as we do not lament that of Claudius), yet also concede a certain fittingness to that outcome. Here, the conflict between 'good' and 'good' resides substantially within the one character: between the public task entailed upon the Prince by his inherited role in the Danish State, and those other impulses and aspirations expressed by (and in) Hamlet for which the state can offer neither place nor public ratification. Such a conflict of 'ethical powers' seems certainly a better way to think of Hamlet's struggle with himself than one characteristic Romantic and post-Romantic version of his plight: virtuous 'individual' versus corrupt 'society'. By 'ethical power', Hegel intends a generalized conception which we, as audience, can respond to as to a *duty*. Hamlet struggles with conflicting duties: one to his familial and political responsibilities, one to a contrasting conception of 'the human' which brings the first into question. Each of these 'ethical powers' is shown to be partial, limited, yet each justified in its own way. Though, again, we may wonder in what 'the triumph of the true' resides. Where is the transcending ethical principle which subsumes each limited good? Hegel's thinking here connects with his historical theory, whereby the 'true ethical Idea' realized itself gradually through progressive human developments, from one civilization to another. Hamlet's sense of duty was directed to political conceptions superseded by the progress of civilization; while his more humane ideas had not yet found their political and social embodiment. The reconciliation of these opposites, Hegel supposes, takes place in our more enlightened minds. Hegel's ideas about 'tragedy' are hardly separable from his philosophical and historical thinking, and here we need also to remember that he was an 'idealist' thinker, proposing that reality is constituted of 'ideas', not 'matter', or material forces and energies. Thus, his 'true ethical Idea' has an existence independent of its historical realizations. The effect of 'tragedy' is that we, as spectators, get access to it, by resolving the ethical conflict presented to us.

But does Hegel's notion about 'tragedy' have any application to *King Lear* (a play which—interestingly enough—he did not write about)? Can you descry a conflict of 'ethical powers', in Hegel's sense?

Neither *Antony and Cleopatra* nor *Hamlet* present us with simple moral conflicts of 'good' against 'evil'. But it seems hard to object to that view of *King Lear*, where the main characters fall unambiguously into a 'good' and a 'bad' group, and such a conflict in Hegel's view cannot be 'tragic', since it is not between 'two equally justified but different ethical powers'. Might there be such a 'tragic' conflict within Lear himself, as we have seen to be the case with Hamlet? That he is torn by internal conflict is evident enough, but can we identify a struggle between one partial 'good' and another? Surely not. Lear's struggle seems to be, unlike Hamlet's, between what *is* good in him, and what *isn't*. He behaved unwisely when he divided the kingdom, self-regardingly when he asked each daughter to woo him for her share of the kingdom, with gross injustice when he rejected Cordelia and banished Kent. There is no evidence in *King Lear* of a conflict between two valid but limited 'goods', so it does seem that Hegel's analysis of 'tragic' conflict does not work for this play.

On pages 42–4, we noted A. C. Bradley's account of *King Lear* as developed in *Shakespearean Tragedy*,* and it will be useful here to consider his general

*Bradley, *op. cit.*

account of 'tragedy', which, as he said, was substantially indebted to Hegel. Indeed, Bradley thought Hegel the only writer since Aristotle to treat the subject of 'tragedy' with original insight. In his essay 'Hegel's Theory of Tragedy', he advanced a number of reservations and additions, and notably in relation to the problem touched on in the preceding paragraph. From the Hegelian point of view *King Lear* raises the same problems as *Macbeth*, and an account of 'tragedy' which cannot apply to *Macbeth*, Bradley argues, must be held unsatisfactory. In the Greek drama that Hegel has primarily in mind, the tragic catastrophe comes about through some *defect* in the tragic protagonist (i.e. '*hamartia*', the Greek term used by Aristotle) which leads to a *crucial error of judgement*. But in Shakespearean drama we are rather aware of some *moral fault* and of the tragic action as engaging a conflict between 'good' and 'evil', *Macbeth* being the most striking case. Bradley's solution is to locate the Hegelian ethical conflict within the tragic protagonist's own special qualities. Macbeth's imaginative power is responsible for the vividness with which he apprehends *both* the satisfactions of kingship, and *equally* of the moral self-destruction which, as he correctly foresees, will follow his crime. The courage that makes him Duncan's bravest and most effective general is the same quality that leads him through one bloody deed after another to the final doomed struggle with Macduff. We therefore view his death as involving the destruction of 'good' as well as of 'evil'. The overriding 'ethical power' affirmed in Malcolm's victory is the re-establishment of a legitimate political authority in the state. But the tragic conflict resides in the self-division whereby Macbeth's potentially 'good' qualities are turned against themselves so as to bring about his destruction. *Macbeth* can thus be seen to illustrate Bradley's general conception of 'tragedy' in that it portrays*

> a self-division and self-waste of spirit, or a division of spirit involving conflict and waste. It is implied in this that on *both* sides in the conflict there is spiritual value. The same idea may be expressed . . . by saying that tragic conflict is one not merely of good with evil, but also, and more essentially, of good with good. Only in saying this, we must be careful to observe that 'good' here means anything that has spiritual value, not moral goodness alone, and that 'evil' has a similarly wide sense.

By this last qualification, Bradley indicates that courage, imagination, and so on (what I have called 'qualities') have intrinsic 'spiritual value', and that he is not invoking some specific moral code, such as might be understood by the terms 'good' and 'evil'. A merely 'evil' character like Regan in *King Lear*, or a merely 'good' one like Banquo in *Macbeth* thus cannot be the focus and occasion of tragic conflict. They are not sufficiently possessed of the qualities that make for 'spiritual value', whose possession in striking degree is the defining characteristic of the tragic protagonist.

Lear's story is tragic, not on account of his moral faults, important though these are in triggering the sequence of events, but in his grandeur, his courage, perhaps above all, in his capacity for radical change. These 'spiritual values' contribute equally to the catastrophe he brings about, to his slide into madness, and to his recovery of 'sanity', the latter on terms so new and strange to the man he was that we think of him as reborn, rather than merely recovered. Lear's struggle is 'tragic' on this account.

Bradley also qualifies Hegel's notion that in viewing the whole action that culminates in tragic catastrophe the audience is reconciled to the destruction of the limited or one-sided 'good' embodied in the tragic protagonist by a vision of profounder and more encompassing 'good'. Bradley approves the notion of reconciliation, and of this coming through an eventual affirmation of 'good'. But

*Bradley, A. C. (1950) *Oxford Lectures on Poetry*, OUP, p. 86.

he conceives the matter differently from Hegel. As he argues in the opening pages of *Shakespearean Tragedy*, we cannot be content with the Hegelian idea that the outcome of a tragic drama affirms some comprehensive principle of ethical justice at work in the universe. This fails to account for the sense of *waste* which tragic drama necessarily produces.

> With Shakespeare, at any rate, the pity and fear which are stirred by the tragic story seem to unite with, and even to merge in, a profound sense of sadness and mystery, which is due to this impression of waste . . . We seem to have before us a type of the mystery of the whole world, the tragic fact which extends far beyond the limits of tragedy. Everywhere . . . we see power, intelligence, life, and glory which astound us and seem to call for our worship. And everywhere we see them perishing, devouring one another and destroying themselves, often with dreadful pain, as though they came into being for no other end. Tragedy is the typical form of this mystery . . .

As you see from this extract,* Bradley belongs with those post-Romantic commentators for whom tragic drama speaks for a general truth about human life. The effect of reconciliation which we gain from tragic drama is directed towards this truth, which is a 'mystery' in the sense that it involves self-contradiction.

> . . . we are left at last with an idea showing two sides or aspects which we can neither separate nor reconcile. The whole or order against which the individual part shows itself powerless seems to be animated by a passion for perfection: we cannot otherwise explain its behaviour towards evil. Yet it appears to engender this evil within itself, and in its effort to overcome and expel it is agonised with pain, and driven to mutilate its own substance, and to lose not only evil but priceless good.

The 'it' of which Bradley writes here† is 'the idea of a moral order' realizing its aims through the actions portrayed in tragic drama, and by 'the individual part' he means the main characters, who carry the action forwards and are destroyed by its outcome. Tragedy, he maintains, does affirm a moral order in the sense that it portrays the destruction of 'evil', but this also involves the destruction of 'good'.

Like Hegel, Bradley is a philosophical 'idealist', as will be evident from his notion of an 'idea of moral order' having real and independent existence. The value of his thinking nevertheless lies, I would wish to suggest, in emphasizing the unresolved contradictions which tragedies leave us with, and to which we assent—not in terms of Hegel's 'true ethical Idea'—but because they speak to our sense of reality. To be more exact, they address both our desire for moral order and our doubt about its existence. But we also need to add that Bradley's terms for expressing this idea are far from satisfactory. He appeals to the notion of a 'moral order [which] . . . appears to engender this evil within itself', and then proceeds to drive it out. A concept of *order* in intrinsic contradiction with itself must be thought—to put it mildly—lacking in lucidity.

Freudian tragedy

Bradley's thinking also demonstrates an assumption (shared by many modern critics) that the conception of human nature to which he appeals is a permanent structure of reality, true for all times and all places, which (like other great artists) Shakespeare addresses with unusual fullness, integrity and insight. We can see in

*Bradley (1957) *op. cit.*, p. 16.
†*Idem*, p. 28.

such a view the persisting influence of neo-classical ideas about life and literature—that *there is a human nature*, already known to great classic writers and dramatists, which it is the task of all writers to perceive and express. It is not possible here to enter into this complex debate, but our knowledge of historical change, of the variety of human languages, of the findings of cultural anthropology, combine to make the assumption of a permanent and ahistoric 'human nature' very difficult to sustain. We surely learn from any engagement with earlier products of our own national culture that its members inhabited the universe in terms evidently distinct from ours, however we may also be able to trace out certain lively continuities. Difference *and* similarity, each as important as the other, is the rule. Conceptions of 'the human' are in continual flux, sometimes slow enough to be all but invisible, sometimes very rapid. But they are never stationary. And what changes them is not 'fate' or 'necessity', so much as human action in time, making and unmaking new cultural forms.

As an example of the way different historical periods evolve different conceptions of a permanent 'human nature', which 'tragedy' reflects, we can turn to Sigmund Freud. We have seen that for Bradley, the tragic fact about human existence lay in the notion of a moral order, both transcending and working within all particular human situations, which was nevertheless mysteriously at war with itself, bringing evil to birth, yet also destroying it. Freud, too, proposed that intrinsic contradiction lay at the centre of our human nature, governing the process of human history. But he conceived the terms of this contradiction very differently from Bradley, not as 'moral' but as 'psychological', a change of conception symptomatic of the differences between our century and Bradley's.

You may remember in Block IV mention of the Freudian interpretation of *Hamlet*. In his seminal *The Interpretation of Dreams* (1900), Freud discussed the play in psychoanalytic terms. The celebrated obscurity of Hamlet's reasons for delaying to revenge his father's murder (argued Freud) derives from the Oedipus Complex, the mental structure common to all human males, which Freud was later to call the 'nuclear complex of the neuroses'.* This condition develops when the small boy begins to regard his father as an all-powerful rival for the love of his mother, prompting dreams and fantasies of killing his father. Yet the father is also admired, and in part identified with, producing in the boy severe mental conflict, which can only be dealt with by repression. The antagonistic feelings towards the father and the sexual attraction towards the mother are banished to the unconscious. Only love and admiration for the father are allowed articulate expression. Such a development is a necessary part of growth from boyhood to adulthood. Hamlet's difficulty was that Claudius, in killing old Hamlet and marrying his wife, enacted the repressed wishes of his nephew. Charged with the task of revenge, Hamlet suffers the partial re-emergence of his own repressed feelings about his father and mother and the guilt and anxiety which is the conscious 'trace' of such repression. This conflict paralyses him. Claudius is a living embodiment of his own infantile fantasies, killer of his father, lover of his mother. To act against him is to act against himself in the most radical way imaginable.

It is on this basis that Freud explains our response to *Hamlet*:†

> The repressed impulse is one of those which are *similarly repressed in all of us, and the repression of which is part and parcel of the foundation of our personal evolution.* It is this repression which is shaken up by the situation in the play. As a result of these two characteristics it is easy for us to recognize ourselves in the hero: we are susceptible to the same conflict as he is . . .

Freud's general explanation of our interest in tragic drama lies here. It represents suffering, from which we nevertheless derive pleasure, because the action is also a

*Freud, S. (1960) *Totem and Taboo*, Routledge and Kegan Paul, p. 129.
†*Idem*, (1953), *Collected Works*, vol. 7, Hogarth Press, p. 309; my italics.

representation, disguised in some degree yet also recognizable, of wishes and desires which have been repressed into the unconscious. Repressed material of this kind must not be allowed full or direct expression. The psychic resistance to its re-emergence must also be respected, otherwise our mental state would become violently disturbed. Freud conceives art as, in a profound manner, compensatory fantasy which must not be permitted to break the bounds separating it from reality. The skilled artist, drawing upon his own fantasy life, understands these limits on the degree to which conflicts repressed into the unconscious may be indirectly and temporarily 'shaken up'. This special knowledge is his distinctive mark.

> He knows how to attach to this reflection of his phantasy-life so strong a stream of pleasure that, for a time at least, the repressions are outbalanced and dispelled by it. When he can do all this, he opens out to all others the way back to the comfort and consolation of their own unconscious sources of pleasure, and so reaps their gratitude and admiration.*

Freud's insistence on *pleasure* surely offers an important advance on earlier thinking about tragic art. Why does what Hegel calls 'the destruction of the best' give *pleasure*? Why should representations of pain and suffering have, in however complex a way, the opposite effect upon us? Not in Freud's view because they offer ethical consolation, but for their indirect connection with forms of instinctual pleasure necessarily repressed in the course of our growth to adult life. Freud's later general thought about culture and society proposed that the very structure of civilized life necessarily incorporates powerful mechanisms for the repression of instinctual pleasure, and that our intuitive knowledge of this means that we live in a state of suppressed resentment of the claims of organized social life. Our assent to these claims, however mature and considered, is always counter-balanced by a keen sense of their high psychic cost in the restriction of our experience of instinctual pleasure. Whatever historical mould has shaped it, human life is characterized by this severe and permanent struggle between what Freud calls 'the pleasure principle', that hard adjustment to the objective conditions of social existence which all civilizations enforce. Lionel Trilling, in his essay on 'Freud and Literature', uses the term 'tragic' of this state of affairs:†

> . . . man (as Freud conceives him) is not to be understood by any simple formula (such as sex) but is rather an inexplicable tangle of culture and biology. And not being simple, he is not simply good; he has . . . a kind of hell within him from which rises everlastingly the impulses which threaten his civilization. He has the faculty of imagining for himself more in the way of pleasure and satisfaction than he can possibly achieve. Everything that he gains he pays for in more than equal coin; compromise and the compounding with defeat constitute his best way of getting through the world. His best qualities are the outcome of a struggle whose outcome is tragic.

Of course, not everyone will agree with Freud's account of the mind, nor indeed with the general view of life which Trilling here summarizes. Yet we can recognize in such an account our distance, in the twentieth century, from Bradley's world. Ethics, in Freudian thought, is a creation of culture, and so in intrinsic opposition to the pleasure-seeking psyche. Bradley conceived a universal moral order obscurely at war with itself, which tragic drama reflects. In Freudian thought, tragic drama is a means of alleviating the psychic wounds caused by our construction of a

*Freud, S. (1922) *Introductory Lectures on Psychoanalysis*, Allen & Unwin, p. 315.
†Trilling, L. (1940) *The Liberal Imagination*, Scribner, p. 57.

moral order and our assent to its imperatives. The irreconcilable character of tragic conflicts may thus be said to speak to the necessary contradictions which Freud discerned within the structure of civilized living.

To return to the plays you have been studying, we have considered *Hamlet* in Freudian terms, but what of the other two tragedies? Take *Antony and Cleopatra* first. Do you see any connection between its subject and Freudian ideas?

You will remember that the play turns on the contrast between 'Roman' and 'Egyptian' values. Broadly speaking, 'Roman' values might be identified with Freud's 'reality principle', the claims of organized social and political life, and 'Egyptian' values with 'the pleasure principle' which makes the desire for pleasure paramount. Each 'principle' strives for complete domination, yet fails to achieve it. The war between them is permanent, and Antony, committed to both sides, is destroyed. Such an account, admittedly, risks turning the play into an unduly simple allegory. Cleopatra, to take the obvious case, is a political figure, as well as 'a lass unparalleled'; and the relationship between her and Antony amounts to much more than hedonistic gratification. Nevertheless, the underlying opposition does bear a striking resemblance to Freud's idea in *Civilization and Its Discontents*, whereby the achievement of civilization (organized society, family life, the state, culture) is only made possible by repressing the demand for immediate instinctual pleasure, that absolute precondition of living organisms.

What of *King Lear* from a Freudian point of view? Freud himself wrote about the play, but he concentrated on the folk-tale element at the centre of all the various versions of the Lear story, that is to say, the love-test imposed by a father on a daughter.* Freud concluded that the inner meaning of the tale was Lear's 'refusal to renounce love, choose death and make friends with the necessity of dying'. You can see the bearing of that on Lear's proclaimed intention to 'Unburdened crawl toward death' (I.1.41), on that *apparent* renunciation of power. Indeed, if we remember the end of the play it seems appropriate to ask whether Lear ever *chooses* death. Does he not fight to the end (contrast Kent)? We can, I think, press the Freudian account further. Lear wants love from his daughters, Cordelia especially: 'I loved her most, and thought to set my rest/On her kind nursery' (I.1.123–4). Think for a moment of the word 'nursery'. Then recall also Cordelia's comment on her sisters' avowals to give their entire love to their father. She points out that as *married* women, they owe at least half their love to their husbands, and adds: 'Sure I shall never marry like my sisters,/To love my father all' (I.1.103–4). Freud's point about Lear refusing to renounce love touches on the erotic element in the love of fathers for daughters (the complement to that of mothers and sons which Freud descried as the underlying structure in *Hamlet*). Lear's rejection (as he sees it) by Cordelia engages this forbidden tangle of feelings and connections. Later, rejected by Gonerill, he denounces her sexuality with ferocious intensity; and in his scene with Gloucester (IV.6) reveals a generalized horror of sexuality in women (IV.6.114–31). If Freud is right in saying that art permits the expression, in disguised form, of repressed desires, then there does seem to be supporting evidence in *King Lear*. As has already been mentioned (pages 28–30), the play engages the contradictory feelings which bind parents and children, of affection and rivalry, of the wish to protect and the determination to replace. Freud sees such contradictions as final, beyond reconciliation, and the value of tragic art in its power to recognize this in a manner acceptable to our everyday consciousness.

*See Bullough, G. (ed.) (1973) *Narrative and Dramatic Sources of Shakespeare*, vol. 7, Routledge and Kegan Paul, p. 271; Freud, S. (1953) *Collected Works*, Hogarth Press, vol. 12, p. 301.

Tragedy and history

In emphatic contrast with Hegel and Bradley, Freud was a *materialist*. He modelled his psychoanalytic investigations of the human mind on the assumptions and procedures of the nineteenth-century sciences. He accepted, that is, that 'reality' was entirely *material*, that ideas had no existence independent of human bodies, or of the human societies that have been created over many thousands of years in the course of human evolution from its earlier, merely animal, condition. Yet an important criticism often advanced against Freud, especially the discussions of religion in *The Future of an Illusion* (1927), of culture in *Civilisation and its Discontents* (1929), of the endless struggle between the pleasure-instinct and the death-instinct in *Beyond the Pleasure Principle* (1920), is that his thinking is 'metaphysical', presupposing a fixed 'human nature', without regard to its specific historical and cultural formations. Thus, it has been argued that Freud's ambitious generalizations about the human psyche derive their only evidential support from the very narrow world of late nineteenth-century European bourgeois society, as known by a small and relatively wealthy segment of that society. More recently, feminists have drawn attention to the patriarchal assumptions in Freud's work, as for example, the key role of the Oedipus Complex in the development of the psyche, which bears primarily on the relation between fathers and sons. In relation to 'tragedy', such objections may serve to remind us that we need to keep historical considerations in mind. This proved difficult with Shakespeare's work because Renaissance ideas about 'tragedy' offered us very little purchase on his plays. The later theorizing we have looked at emphasizes the notion of intrinsic and unresolved conflict and faces the problem of why such representations can be a source of 'pleasure', and in these ways engages more directly than Renaissance ideas with our experiences of *Antony and Cleopatra*, *Hamlet* and *King Lear*. Holding to this clue, let us return to a more historically-grounded discussion.

You will recall from the earlier discussion of John F. Danby's account of the idea of 'Nature' in *King Lear* (pages 45–50), which discussed three conflicting definitions: Lear's idea of a social and political order sanctioned by the gods, Edmund's of a thrusting amoral individualism, and the idea, associated with Cordelia, of a 'nature' in which the struggle for power had no place. You will recall, too, that these ideas had their roots in actual historical developments. Lear's 'Nature' corresponded to medieval-feudal conceptions in which society was ordered by a hierarchy of 'estates' bound to each other by reciprocal duties and responsibilities culminating in the King, who was in his turn responsible to God. Edmund's 'Nature' looked forward to the secular Hobbesian view of 'naturally' warring individuals whom only the arbitrary imposition of superior power could bring into cohesive social relationships. While the third idea, the utopian possibility of egalitarian, mutually-supportive social relationships had its roots in Christian-communist thinking, and was to emerge in earnest on the political scene during the Civil War. Danby suggested that in these ways *King Lear* engaged with historical processes at work in the society of Shakespeare's time. Now Marxist thinking about 'tragedy' insists upon the relationship of its particular forms (Greek, Renaissance, Ibsenite, etc.) to the historical context of such forms. Marx, in general, argued that Hegel's analysis of historical process as a conflict of ideas, or spiritual forces, should be turned on its head. These conflicts of ideas should be rather seen as conflicts of social and political forces, to be concretely observed in the workings of particular institutions, legal arrangements, ownership of property, in every aspect of social life, not excluding the arts. Tragedies thus reflect, not conflicts of ethical ideas, but of specific social and historical forces. Raymond Williams summarizes this view as follows:*

*Williams, Raymond, *op. cit.*, p. 35.

> The [Hegelian] conflict of ethical forces, and their resolution by a higher force, were seen in social and historical terms. Social development was seen as necessarily contradictory in character, and tragedy occurs at those points where the conflicting forces must, by their inner nature, take action, and carry the conflict through to a transformation . . .
>
> Renaissance tragedy has been seen as the embodiment of the conflict between a dying feudalism and the new individualism. It is not eternal justice, in Hegel's sense, that is affirmed in the tragic issue, but rather the general movement of history, in a series of decisive transformations of society. Not all conflicts of this kind lead to tragedy. There is only tragedy when each side finds it necessary to act, and refuses to give way.

Danby's account of *King Lear* is not Marxist, but in identifying the play's basic source of conflict as a matter of complex *social* ideas (as these are represented by the different definitions of 'Nature') it has some resemblance to it. Remember here his assertion that to adopt one definition rather than another of an idea as wide-ranging as 'Nature' is no mere intellectual act, and in this, Shakespeare's play clearly supports him. The different definitions directly lead those who adopt them to different kinds of behaviour, different conceptions of how to act (and react) to the crisis which Lear's abdication brings about.

Nevertheless, looking back at Williams' description of the Marxist view of tragedy, does *King Lear* provide an effective illustration, or does it differ in some way?

It seems to me to have suggestive application to *King Lear*, but we would surely need to add that the play hardly presents 'the general movement of history'. If Lear and his court, and Lear's ideas about society, are (broadly speaking) feudal, and in that sense, speak for dying social forms, we do not gain any impression of the new *social forms*, which (historically speaking) replaced them. Edmund's 'individualism', though contemptuously dismissive of the structure of 'natural' (i.e. feudal) obligations, is nevertheless not linked with any alternative social embodiment. If Edmund had defeated Edgar, married one of the sisters, disposed of Albany, and himself become King, we could imagine him quite easily, even if cynically, defending his claim to obedience in traditional terms. His thinking about 'Nature' may indeed point to later ideas which *had* direct social relevance, but the play itself provides no direct reflection of that relevance. If we are looking for evidence of irreconcilable conflicts in the play, these exist rather at the level of ideology. Thus, on the one hand, there is Lear's ideal conception of 'natural' duties and responsibilities, the structure which sanctions his kingly authority; but on the other, there is the discovery of how little that corresponded to the real world: the helplessness and misery of the poor, the corruption of justice by the rich, the identification of law with power (e.g. Gonerill's 'the laws are mine', V.3.156), the impotence of the ideas associated with Cordelia to realize themselves, save in the most vulnerable personal terms. Setting these conflicts before us the play simply leaves them unresolved. To quote again the answer of the soldier to Edmund's orders that he kill Lear and Cordelia:

> I cannot draw a cart nor eat dried oats;
> If it be man's work, I'll do't.
>
> (V.3.39–40)

Which he does, as we soon discover. So, *was* it 'man's work'? The play both presents, and challenges, just this possibility, leaving the question for us to answer. And this method seems characteristic of its treatment of social issues. The specific historical dimension is touched on, but hardly, in the Marxist sense, fully explored.

Let us pursue now the historical issue in closer relation to the dramatic structure of the play. In considering 'What sort of comedy is *Measure for Measure*?' (Block V, pp. 57–65), we found that Shakespeare drew upon popular Elizabethan dramatic practice. His own comedies, *A Midsummer Night's Dream*, *Twelfth Night*, and others, embody the festive and anarchic spirit of popular Elizabethan holidays and the games and entertainments which celebrated them. His use of the 'upper' and 'lower' acting areas of the public-theatre stages, it has been argued, provided the theatrical means for incorporating two distinct social strata: the rulers and gentry involved in the romantic or heroic action, and the ordinary people with their different point of view about that action. Drawing on such traditions (so I suggested) in *Measure for Measure*, Shakespeare presented not a unified over-view of the theme, resolving into a complex whole the different points of view which the play expresses on the main story, but unresolved conflicts, the play's power lying precisely in their not being resolved. Now we have seen that Sidney, in the remark about 'mungrell Tragy-comedie' cited above (p. 79), designated this mixture of social strata as a principal fault, because 'Clownes' have no place in the 'maiesticall matters' proper to tragedies. And we also remember that Shakespeare's tragedies often involve exactly that kind of dissonance: the Porter in *Macbeth*, Hamlet's adoption of a Fool's role, the Clown admitted into Cleopatra's final scene. The question now to press is: why? Why does Shakespeare exploit in his tragedies methods and effects characteristic of his comedies? We have seen already (pp. 17–20) that in *King Lear* the Fool has a key part in the early acts. The Fool is one of Shakespeare's vehicles for bringing to bear on Lear's predicament a point of view entirely alien to the world of Lear's court. The Fool is, formally, a sort of member of that court. But his style of speech, gnomic riddling, satiric, sprinkled with popular jokes and songs, draws upon experiences of life from which the court is protected. The Fool is 'oppositional'—not boldly like Kent, or silently like Cordelia. His is the opposition of the powerless. It is sly, indirect, wrapped in ambiguity and doubleness.

> *Fool* That sir which serves and seeks for gain,
> And follows but for form,
> Will pack when it begins to rain,
> And leave thee in the storm;
> But I will tarry, the fool will stay,
> And let the wise man fly,
> The knave turns fool that runs away;
> The fool no knave, perdy.
> *Kent* Where learned you this, Fool?
> *Fool* Not i'the stocks, fool.
>
> (II.4.74–83)

The Fool learned in Lear's court (what Lear himself only recognizes when, taken captive with Cordelia, he says that 'we'll wear out,/In a walled prison, packs and sects of great ones/That ebb and flow by the moon' (V.3.17–19)) the key to the situation Lear finds himself in: he no longer wields any political power. He also learned that if you challenge the powerful you end where Kent now is: in the stocks, or worse. Such an exchange, located in the 'down-stage' acting position, in semi-direct address to the audience, would be quickly read for that meaning. But there is a further cryptic meaning. 'Wisdom' is *prudential*; it lies in self-preservation, keeping in with the powerful. 'Folly' is not to realize this, or to choose differently. The last two lines then gloss this shrewd sense of political reality with a covert judgement. The fool who stays loyal is not a knave, whereas the prudential man who flies from trouble is; and, moreover, in a *different sense*, he is a self-deceiving fool locked into a system of endless treachery, double-dealing, struggling for gain, which by its very premises can hold no promise of stability. Such utterances both recognize the truth about power politics—a truth which Lear at this stage cannot grasp because the ingrained pattern of his thinking makes the power structure he has headed 'natural' to him—and yet also undercut it with a point of view entirely alien. Who *is* the 'fool'? The prudential man says, 'Somebody like Kent who can't read the political situation rightly, defies the King to no purpose, and is banished for his pains.' The Fool gives a different answer: 'The prudential man is a fool, because he fails to see the self-destructive character of the system he upholds.' Oswald is that kind of fool. As Empson has shown in his brilliant essay 'Fool in Lear'* the word engages opposite meanings, which cannot be reconciled—though they can be chosen between. It defines 'the real' in opposed ways, each of which leads to its own distinct map of the world of social relationships. The Fool's role in the play is to sharpen our sense of these oppositions, which lead directly to the painful conflicts worked out in each of the plots. That is the sense in which he contributes to a general effect which also derives from many other elements in the play.

We entered on this discussion of the Fool in *King Lear* in an attempt to discover why, in this tragedy (as in others, if less strikingly), Shakespeare had developed to such an extraordinary degree a technique and structure characteristic of his comedies. Can we conclude that it provides him with a theatrical means for presenting unresolvable conflicts? When we remember that the Fool's style and presence belong to the 'popular' end of the social spectrum, that his sardonic wit is in the non-mimetic, anti-illusionist mode, that it is at first in *him* that Lear begins to see the world from the point of view of the 'Poor naked wretches ... That bide the pelting of this pitiless storm' (III.4.28–9), and to break loose from the thinking that has governed his kingly existence, we can see that such conflicts amount to more than the profound word-play, which attention to the mere term 'fool' might have implied. Put briefly, perhaps crudely, the Fool is the means whereby Shakespeare juxtaposes two irreconcilable political experiences: of being *inside* the world of power and privilege, and of being *outside* it, and so at its mercy. This is an experience which the 'good' characters (Lear, Gloucester, Edgar, Cordelia, with Kent the only exception) all undergo in various degrees of intensity, and with various effects. I would like to suggest, then, that we confront here one central engagement between *King Lear* and the history of its own time, which is nevertheless not confined to that time, and which bears crucially upon its being a 'tragedy'.

The Fool, end of V.3. (Kozintsev's King Lear.) *(Courtesy of National Film Archive/Stills Library)*

*Empson, W. (1951) *The Structure of Complex Words*, Chatto & Windus, pp. 125–57.

The dead Lear, V.3. 'Exeunt with a dead march'. (*Kozintsev's* King Lear.) (*Courtesy of National Film Archive/Stills Library*)

We saw on pages 10–13, that the play begins by opening up a conflict between the category of the *political* and the category of the *moral*, and this is a more general way of stating the issue raised by means of the Fool. Now, there is a sense in which *King Lear* presents a moral conflict between 'good' and 'evil'. The characterization of both parties is defined largely in terms of black and white oppositions, rather than complexly-defined personalities. The story, too, has its straightforward moral aspect. The 'good' are first defeated with cruel thoroughness, and the 'evil' hold sway; but then the 'good' revive and, in the persons of Edgar and Albany, triumph over the 'evil'. Edgar's emblematic duel with Edmund may be seen as summarizing this pattern. But cutting against this schema is a different pattern, and without it we would not have a 'tragedy', only a violent political melodrama. This derives from the *system of power*, of the ambition for it, of its political necessity, of its amoral logic. Edmund is its chief spokesman, with the curiously attractive character of those explicit 'villains' we find in Shakespeare's plays. Considered from his brother's or father's angle, both of whom he treats atrociously, we will think Edmund 'evil'. But considered from his own? 'Well then,/*Legitimate* Edgar, I must have your *land*' (I.2.15–16). My point is not just that 'there is something to be said for Edmund', that 'he has some positive qualities', that 'remembering his illegitimate birth, we sympathize in some degree with his ambitions', though Shakespeare presents him in a way to attract such feelings. It is rather that the system of 'legitimacy', the social set-up Edmund finds himself struggling with, is presented as a truth about the world, which carries its own implications. I have called Edmund the play's materialist (above, p. 39), meaning that he sees through the mystifications which gloss the system of 'legitimacy' with 'virtuous seeming'. An outsider, he insists upon a real aspect of the world of the 'legitimate' insiders. This is indeed how the political world works—it is not 'good'; it results in much 'evil'. Yet, as a system it is not presented as 'evil', but as a reality beyond the reach of moral judgements.

Or again, consider Cordelia. Her flat rejection of the terms offered by her father is impressive, but as many critics have pointed out, such morally absolute commitment prompts searching questions. Shakespeare, as it were, asks us to see all round Cordelia's position. Certainly, it is 'good', but so presented as to invite our awareness of what it excludes: tact, prudence (not in its pejorative sense as narrow self-seeking, but as implying good judgement of consequences), perhaps imaginative insight into her father's nature (an insight not denied to her coldly shrewd sisters). Critics who descry in Cordelia's 'Nothing' an attitude tainted by immature self-righteousness, or by Lear-like stubborness surely miss the point as completely as those who wish only to praise her 'goodness'. Cordelia is 'good'. What the play shows is the collision of 'goodness' with differently impelled commitments such as Edmund's.

The point can be made on a larger scale by considering the interrelationship of power and morality which the play repeatedly puts before us. We see the awful misuse of power in individual cases (Gonerill and Regan mistreating their father, Edmund betraying his), and the mad Lear generalizes the case to suggest that the very structure of political power is intrinsically evil, subverting law and morality to cruel and oppressive purposes. But how do we read Lear's speech to Cordelia expressing a total rejection of secular power of any kind (V.3.8–19)? Is this an ultimately moral position against which all other statements and positions can be tested and found wanting? Some critics read it that way. Yet what is its consequence? One is Cordelia's death. From elsewhere in the play, we know that the powerless (i.e. the poor) do not enjoy the happy condition that Lear imagines might be his and his daughter's in prison. The task of the survivors is, exactly, the restoration of the shattered political structure. 'Friends of my soul,' says Albany to Edgar and Kent, 'you twain,/Rule in this realm, and the gored state sustain' (V.3.317–18). This is considerably more than saying 'life must go on'. What must go on is *politics*, the assertion of power by means of the institutions necessary to a state. We are back in the world of Edmund's 'legitimacy'. In sum what makes *King Lear* a 'tragedy', as distinct from a tale of the conflict of 'good, with 'evil', is that it represents this irreconcilability of the political and the moral, each idea realized as a specific social and human sphere of action.

We can now perhaps link this theme to Shakespeare's time, and again to our own. Historical periods in which the basic political structures are undergoing serious change, or at least felt to be under challenge, will have the effect of emphasizing this contradiction between the political and the moral, whereas in periods when the political structures are stable this contradiction remains hidden. When the system of 'legitimacy' is indeed generally felt to *be* legitimate, or when those who might question its legitimacy have no voice, then its relation with morality is not *experienced* as problematic. The Nahum Tate version of *King Lear* (no Fool, Cordelia and Edgar married, the virtuous finally triumphant, all the play's conflicts *resolved*) belongs to such a period. The later recovery of Shakespeare's *King Lear*, and the high esteem in which it is now held, then turn out to be signs of our own history, of our own modern sense of the clash between the political and moral. Here, at any rate, is one way in which the 'tragedy' of *King Lear* speaks to us with a power that few other plays can equal.

Conclusion

In this last part, we have surveyed some accounts of 'tragedy', partly for the intrinsic importance of the subject, partly as a way of prompting comparisons and contrasts between the three tragic plays studied in the course. Rather than these general discussions, you may find it more helpful to read further amongst specific accounts of *King Lear* (as of other plays). Theoretical discussion in any case is always best pursued in relation to the widest possible knowledge of particular plays.

But what needs to be remembered is that we can never proceed *without* theory, in the sense of governing concepts which enable us to interpret and discuss texts in the first place. The most detailed interpretation of any text will be dependent, in some degree, on theory, or more probably, on a 'mix' of theories, often not clearly distinguished or grasped. Our discussion of different theories of 'tragedy', concluding in some specific suggestions of my own about what makes *King Lear* a 'tragedy', can provide no more than a beginning, but I hope will have served to underline the presence of 'theory' at some level in any discussion of these plays.

As to *King Lear* itself, and as perhaps for anybody writing about it, my overall sense is of how much might be said, how much of value and insight has been said by others, and of how marginal to the experience of the play, writing *about* it—and indeed *writing* about it—turns out to be. The distinguished Shakespearean scholar Clifford Leech, in speaking of the effect of seeing the play, tells this anecdote:*

> I can remember a performance of *Lear* at Stratford-upon-Avon which I saw in company with a colleague. It was our custom to go for a walk in the night-air after visiting the theatre, and I suggested we should do it on this occasion. 'Yes', he said, 'a walk, but I don't want to talk.' He was right of course, and we did not talk though we walked for a few miles in the night . . . We were not feeling free from emotion, we were not frightened, we had not been impelled to take up arms. Our condition was one of tension still, of feeling a need to re-orientate but with no specific programme suggested to us. 'This is how things are' is an inadequate way of suggesting the kind of cognition we experienced. Rather, 'this is what we have to face, and we do not know, and we cannot quarrel with the dramatist for not telling us, how to face it.'

Perhaps you have not been able to see a performance of the play, or one of the films that has been made from it? But how did you feel when you had finished reading it? Does the experience of Leech and his friend strike a chord for you?

*Leech, C. (1969) *Tragedy*, Methuen, p. 50.

Further reading

There are many good critical discussions of *King Lear*, as a whole, and of various aspects of it. You might want to read some of the accounts of the play I have referred to in Part Two. An excellent selection of material is available in the Macmillan Casebook on *King Lear* (1972) edited by Frank Kermode. His introduction is particularly helpful in addressing directly the relation of each interpretation to the text itself. The essay by Maynard Mack, 'Actors and Redactors', surveys the history of different productions. Robert B. Heilman's 'The Unity of *King Lear*' sets out an argument to which he also devoted a whole book *This Great Stage* (1948). W. R. Elton's 'Double Plot in *King Lear*' is a valuable essay on the interrelationship of the two 'stories'. Kermode also provides a select bibliography.

Those of you who have an interest in textual study should know that opinion has swung round to the view that the Folio text of *King Lear* represents a second version of the play, Shakespeare's revision of the Quarto text. This view is set out by Stanley Wells in 'The Division of the Kingdoms, Shakespeare's two versions of *King Lear*', *Oxford Shakespeare Studies*, 1983.

On the subject of tragedy, you could usefully turn to the title of that name, by Clifford Leech, in the Critical Idiom series published by Methuen (1969). As well as Leech's own stimulating and ranging account, there is an excellent annotated list of further reading on the subject. Raymond Williams's *Modern Tragedy* (1960) includes a compressed survey of different conceptions of tragedy with some pages on the Renaissance idea. Lionel Trilling's essay 'Freud and Literature' in *The Liberal Imagination* (1950) would also be worth turning to, though the scope goes beyond tragic drama. A particularly fine essay on *Hamlet* and *King Lear* and the nature of the tragic hero is by Arnold Kettle in *Shakespeare in a Changing World* (1964). For some further titles, see *A New Companion to Shakespeare Studies*, (1971) in the reading list for chapter ten.

Always remember though that reading about *King Lear* or 'tragedy' should go hand-in-hand with reading, and re-reading—and wherever possible, seeing productions of—the play itself.

Appendix
Two principal sources for King Lear

Selections from Raphael Holinshed

The Chronicles of England, Scotland, and Ireland

Leir the son of Baldud was admitted ruler over the Britains, in the year of the world 3105, at what time Joas reigned in Juda. This Leir was a prince of right noble demeanor, governing his land and subjects in great wealth. He made the town of Caerleir now called Leicester, which standeth upon the river of Sore. It is written that he had by his wife three daughters without other issue, whose names were Gonorilla, Regan, and Cordeilla, which daughters he greatly loved, but specially Cordeilla the youngest far above the two elder. When this Leir therefore was come to great years, & began to wax unweildy through age, he thought to understand the affections of his daughters towards him, and prefer her whom he best loved, to the succession over the kingdom. Whereupon he first asked Gonorilla the eldest, how well she loved him: who calling her gods to record, protested that 'she loved him more than her own life, which by right and reason should be most dear unto her'. With which answer the father being well pleased, turned to the second, and demanded of her how well she loved him: who answered (confirming her sayings with great oaths) that she loved him 'more than tongue could express, and far above all other creatures of the world'.

Then called he his youngest daughter Cordeila before him, and asked of her what account she made of him, unto whom she made this answer as followeth: 'Knowing the great love and fatherly zeal that you have always borne towards me (for the which I may not answer you otherwise than I think and as my conscience leadeth me) I protest unto you, that I have loved you ever, and will continually (while I live) love you as my natural father. And if you would more understand of the love that I bear you, ascertain yourself, that so much as you have, so much you are worth, and so much I love you, and no more.' The father being nothing content with this answer, married his two eldest daughters, the one unto Henninus, the duke of Cornwall, and the other unto Maglanus, the duke of Albania, betwixt whom he willed and ordained that his land should be divided after his death, and the one half thereof immediately should be assigned to them in hand: but for the third daughter Cordeilla he reserved nothing.

Nevertheless it fortuned that one of the princes of Gallia (which now is called France), whose name was Aganippus, hearing of the beauty, womanhood, and good conditions of the said Cordeilla, desired to have her in marriage, and sent over to her father, requiring that he might have her to wife; to whom answer was made, that he might have his daughter, but as for any dower he could have none, for all was promised and assured to her other sisters already. Aganippus notwithstanding this answer of denial to receive anything by way of dower with Cordeilla, took her to wife, only moved thereto (I say) for respect of her person and amiable virtues. This Aganippus was one of the twelve kings that ruled Gallia in those days, as in British history it is recorded. But to proceed.

After that Leir was fallen into age, the two dukes that had married his two eldest daughters, thinking it long ere the government of the land did come to their hands, arose against him in armour, and refit from him the governance of the land, upon conditions to be continued for term of life: by the which he was put to his portion, that is, to live after a rate assigned to him for the maintenance of his estate, which in process of time was diminshed as well by Maglanus as by Henninus. But the greatest grief that Leir took, was to see the unkindness of his daughters, which seemed to think that all was too much which their father had, the same being never so little: in so much that going from the one to the other, he was brought to that misery, that scarcely they would allow him one to wait upon him.

In the end, such was the unkindness, or (as I may say) the unnaturalness which he found in his two daughters, notwithstanding their fair and pleasant words uttered in time past, that being constrained of necessity, he fled the land, & sailed into Gallia, there to seek some comfort of his youngest daughter Cordeilla, whom beforetime he hated. The lady Cordeilla hearing that he was arrived in poor estate, she first sent to him privily a certain sum of money to apparel himself withal, and to retain a certain number of servants that might attend upon him in honourable wise, as appertained to the estate which he had borne: and then so accompanied, she appointed him to come to the court, which he did, and was so joyfully, honorably, and lovingly received, both by his son-in-law Aganippus, and also by his daughter Cordeilla, that his hear was greatly comforted: for he was no less honored, than if he had been king of the whole country himself.

Now when he had informed his son-in-law and his daughter in what sort he had been used by his other daughters, Aganippus caused a mighty army to be put in a readiness, and likewise a great navy of ships to be rigged, to pass over into Britain with Leir his father-in-law, to see him again restored to his kingdom. It was accorded, that Cordeilla should also go with him to take possession of the land, the which he promised to leave unto her, as the rightful inheritor after his decease, notwithstanding any former grant made to her sisters or to their husbands in any manner of wise.

Hereupon, when this army and navy of ships were ready, Leir and his daughter Cordeilla with her husband took the sea, and arriving in Britain, fought with their enemies, and discomfited them in battle, in the which Maglanus and Henninus were slain; and then was Leir restored to his kingdom, which he ruled after this by the space of two years, and then died, forty years after he first began to reign. His body was buried at Leicester in a vault under the channel of the river of Sore beneath the town.

Sir Philip Sidney from Arcadia

The pitiful state, and story of the Paphlagonian unkind King, and his kind son, first related by the son, then by the blind father.

It was in the kingdom of Galacia, the season being (as in the depth of winter) very cold, and as then suddenly grown to so extreme and foul a storm, that never any winter (I think) brought forth a fouler child: so that the Princes were even compelled by the hail, that the pride of the wind blew into their faces, to seek some shrouding place within a certain hollow rock offering it unto them, they made it their shield against the tempest's fury. And so staying there, till the violence thereof was passed, they heard the speech of a couple, who not perceiving them (being hid within that rude canopy) held a strange and pitiful disputation which made them step out; yet in such sort, as they might see unseen. There they perceived an aged man, and a young, scarcely come to the age of a man, both poorly arrayed, extremely weather-beaten; the old man blind, the young man leading him: and yet through all those miseries, in both these seemed to appear a kind of nobleness, not suitable to that affliction. But the first words they heard, were these of the old man. Well Leonatus (said he) since I cannot persuade thee to lead me to that which should end my grief, & thy trouble, let me now entreat thee to leave me: fear not, my misery cannot be greater than it is, & nothing doth become me but misery; fear not the danger of my blind steps. I cannot fall worse than I am. And do not I pray thee, do not obstinately continue to infect thee with my wretchedness. But fly, fly from this region, only worthy of me. Dear father (answered he) do not take away from me the only remnant of my happiness: while I have power to do you service, I am not wholly miserable. Ah my son (said he, and with that he groaned, as if sorrow strove to break his heart), how evil fits it me to have such a son, and how much doth thy kindness upbraid my wickedness? These doleful speeches, and some others to like purpose (well showing they had not been borne to the fortune they were in,) moved the Princes to go out unto them, and ask the younger what they were? Sirs (answered he, with a good grace, and made the more agreeable by a certain noble kind of piteousness) I see well you are strangers, that know not our misery so well here known, that no man dare know, but that we must be miserable. Indeed our state is such, as though nothing is so needful unto us as pity, yet nothing is more dangerous unto us, than to make ourselves so known as may stir pity. But your presence promiseth, that cruelty shall not overrun hate. And if it did, in truth our state is sunk below the degree of fear.

This old man (whom I lead) was lately rightful Prince of this country of Paphlagonia, by the hard-hearted ungratefulness of a son of his, deprived, not only of his kingdom (whereof no foreign forces were ever able to spoil him) but of his sight, the riches which Nature grants to the poorest creatures. Whereby, & by other his unnatural dealings, he hath been driven to such grief, as even now he would have had me to have led him to the top of this rock, thence to cast himself headlong to death: and so would have made me (who received my life of him) to be the worker of his destruction. But noble Gentlemen (said he) if either of you have a father, and feel what dutiful affection is engraffed in a son's heart, let me entreat you to convey this afflicted Prince to some place of rest & security. Amongst your worthy acts it shall be none of the least, that a King, of such might and fame, and so unjustly oppressed, is in any sort by you relieved.

But before they could make him answer, his father began to speak, Ah my son (said he) how evil an Historian are you, that leave out the chief knot of all the discourse! my wickedness, my wickedness. And if thou doest it to spare my ears, (the only sense now left me proper for knowledge) assure thy self thou dost mistake me. And I take witness of that sun which you see (with that he cast up his blind eyes, as if he would hunt for light,) and wish myself in worse case than I do wish myself, which is as evil as may be, if I speak untruly; that nothing is so welcome to my thoughts, as the publishing of my shame. Therefore know you Gentlemen (to whom from my heart I wish that it may not prove ominous foretoken of misfortune to have met with such a miser as I am) that whatsoever my son (O God, that truth binds me to reproach him with the name of my son) hath said, is true. But besides those truths this also is true, that having had in lawful marriage, of a mother fit to bear royal children, this son (such one as partly you see, and better shall know by my short declaration) and so enjoyed the expectations in the world of him, till he was grown to justify their expectations (so as I needed envy no father for the chief comfort of mortality, to leave another oneself after me) I was carried by a bastard son of mine (if at least I be bound to believe the words of that base woman my concubine, his mother) first to mislike, then to hate, lastly to destroy, to do my best to destroy, this son (I think you think) undeserving destruction. What ways he used to bring me to it, if I should tell you, I should tediously trouble you with as much poisonous hypocrisy, desperate fraud, smooth malice, hidden ambition, & smiling envy, as in any living person could be harbored. But I list it not, no remembrance, (no, of naughtiness) delights me, but mine own; & me thinks, the accusing his trains might in some manner excuse my fault, which certainly I loathe to do. But the conclusion is, that I gave order to some servants of mine, whom I thought as apt for such charities as myself, to lead him out into a forest, & there to kill him.

But those thieves (better natured to my son than myself) spared his life, letting him go, to learn to live poorly: which he did, giving himself to be a private soldier, in a country hereby. But as he was ready to be greatly advanced for some noble pieces of service which he did, he heard news of me: who (drunk in my affection to that unlawful and unnatural son of mine) suffered myself so to be governed by him, that all favors and punishments passed by him, all offices, and places of importance, distributed to his favorites; so that ere I was aware, I had left myself nothing but the name of a King: which he shortly weary of too, with many indignities (if anything may be called an indignity, which was laid upon me) threw me out of my seat, and put out my eyes; and then (proud in his tyranny) let me go, neither imprisoning, nor killing me: but rather delighting to make me feel my misery; misery indeed, if ever there were any: full of wretchedness, fuller of disgrace, and fullest of guiltiness. And as he came to the crown by so unjust means, as unjustly he kept it, by force of stranger soldiers in citadels, the nests of tyranny, & murderers of liberty; disarming all his own countrymen, that no man durst show himself a well-wisher of mine: to say the truth (I think) few of them being so (considering my cruel folly to my good son, and foolish kindness to my unkind bastard): but if there were any who fell to pity of so great a fall, and had yet any sparks of unstained duty left in them towards me, yet durst they not show it, scarcely with giving me alms at their doors; which yet was the only sustenance of my distressed life, nobody daring to show so much charity, as to lend me a hand to guide my dark steps: Till this son of mine (God knows, worthy of a more virtuous, and more fortunate father) forgetting my abominable wrongs, not recking danger, & neglecting the present good way he was in doing himself good, came hither to do this kind office you see him perform towards me, to my unspeakable grief; not only because his kindness is a glass even to my blind eyes, of my naughtiness, but that above all griefs, it grieves me he should desperately adventure the loss of his soul-deserving life for mine, that yet owe more to fortune for my deserts, as if he would carry mud in a chest of crystal. For well I know, he that now reigneth, how much soever (and with good reason) he despiseth me, of all men despised; yet he will not let slip any advantage to make away him, whose just title (ennobled by courage and goodness) may one day shake the seat of a never secure tyranny. And for this cause I craved of him to lead me to the top of this rock, indeed I must confess, with meaning to free him from so serpentine a companion as I am. But he finding what I purposed, only therein since he was born, showed himself disobedient unto me. And now Gentlemen, you have the true story, which I pray you publish to the world, that my mischievous proceedings may be the glory of his filial piety, the only reward now left for so great a merit. And if it may be, let me obtain that of you, which my son denies me: for never was there more pity in saving any, than in ending me; both because therein my agonies shall end, and so shall you preserve this excellent young man, who else willfully follows his own ruin.

The matter in itself lamentable, lamentably expressed by the old Prince (which needed not take to himself the gestures of pity, since his face could not put off the marks thereof) greatly moved the two Princes to compassion, which could not stay in such hearts as theirs without seeking remedy. But by and by the occasion was presented: for Plexirtus (so was the bastard called) came thither with forty horse, only of purpose to murder this brother; of whose coming he had soon advertisement, and thought no eyes of sufficient credit in such a matter, but his own; and therefore came himself to be actor, and spectator. And as soon as he came, not regarding the weak (as he thought) guard of but two men, commanded some of his followers to set their hands to his, in the killing of Leonatus. But the young Prince (though not otherwise armed but with a sword) how falsely soever he was dealt with by others, would not betray himself: but bravely drawing it out, made the death of the first that assaulted him, warn his fellows to come more warily after him. But then Pyrocles and Musidorus were quickly become parties (so just a defense deserving as much as old friendship) and so did behave them among that company (more injurious, than valiant) that many of them lost their lives for their wicked master.

Yet perhaps had the number of them at last prevailed, if the King of Pontus (lately by them made so) had not come unlooked for to their succor. Who (having had a dream which had fixed his imagination vehemently upon some great danger presently to follow those two Princes whom he most dearly loved) was come in all haste, following as well as he could their track with a hundred horses in that country, which he thought (considering who then reigned) a fit place enough to make the stage of any tragedy.

But then the match had been so ill made for Plexirtus, that his ill-led life, &

worse-gotten honor should have tumbled together to destruction; had there not come in Tydeus & Telenor, with forty or fifty in their suit, to the defense of Plexirtus. These two were brothers, of the noblest house of that country, brought up from their infancy with Plexirtus: men of such prowess, as not to know fear in themselves, and yet to teach it others that should deal with them; for they had often made their lives triumph over most terrible dangers; never dismayed and ever fortunate; and truly no more settled in their valor, than disposed to goodness and justice, if either they had lighted on a better friend, or could have learned to make friendship a child, and not the father of virtue. But bringing up (rather than choice) having first knit their minds unto him (indeed crafty enough, either to hide his faults, or never to show them, but when they might pay home) they willingly hide his faults, or never to show them, but when they might pay home) they willingly held out the course, rather to satisfy him, than all the world; and rather to be good friends, than good men: so as though they did not like the evil he did, yet they liked him that did the evil; and though not councillors of the offense, yet protectors of the offender. Now they having heard of this sudden going out, with so small a company, in a country full of evil-wishing minds toward him (though they knew not the cause) followed him; till they found him in such case as they were to venture their lives, or else he to lose his: which they did with such force of mind and body, that truly I may justly say, Pyrocles & Musidorus had never till then found any, that could make them so well repeat their hardest lesson in the feats of arms. And briefly so they did, that if they overcame not yet were they not overcome, but carried away that ungrateful master of theirs to a place of security; howsoever the Princes labored to the contary. But this matter being thus far begun, it became not the constancy of the Princes so to leave it; but in all haste making forces both in Pontus and Phrygia, they had in few days, left him but only that one strong place where he was. For fear having been the only knot that had fastened his people unto him, that once untied by a greater force, they all scattered from him; like so many birds, whose cage had been broken.

In which season the blind King (having in the chief city of his realm, set the crown upon his son Leonatus' head) with many tears (both of joy and sorrow) setting forth to the whole people, his own fault & his son's virtue, after he had kissed him, and forced his son to accept honor of him (as of his new-become subject) even in a moment died, as it should seem: his heart broken with unkindness & affliction, stretched so far beyond his limits with this excess of comfort, as it was able no longer to keep safe his royal spirits. But the new King (having no less lovingly performed all duties to him dead, than alive) pursued on the siege of his unnatural brother, as much for the revenge of his father, as for the establishing of his own quiet. In which siege truly I cannot but acknowledge the prowess of those two brothers, than whom the Princes never found in all their travel two men of greater ability to perform, nor of abler skill for conduct.

But Plexirtus finding, that if nothing else, famine would at last bring him to destruction, thought better by humbleness to creep, where by pride he could not march. For certainly so had nature formed him, & the exercise of craft conformed him to all turnings of sleights, that though no man had less goodness in his soul than he, no man could better find the places whence arguments might grow of goodness to another: though no man felt less pity, no man could tell better how to stir pity: no man more impudent to deny, where proofs were not manifest; no man more ready to confess with a repenting manner of aggravating his own evil, where denial would but make the fault fouler. Now he took this way, that having gotten a passport for one (that pretended he would put Plexirtus alive into his hands) to speak with the King his brother, he himself (though much against the minds of the valiant brothers, who rather wished to die in brave defense) with a rope about his neck, barefooted, came to offer himself to the discretion of Leonatus. Where what submission he used, how cunningly in making greater the fault he made the faultiness the less, how artificially he could set out the torments of his own conscience, with the burdensome cumber he had found of his ambitious desires, how finely seeming to desire nothing but death, as ashamed to live, he begged life in the refusing it, I am not cunning enough to be able to express: but so fell out of it, that though at first sight Leonatus saw him with no other eye, than as the murderer of his father; & anger already began to paint revenge in many colors, ere long he had not only gotten pity, but pardon, and if not an excuse of the fault past, yet an opinion of future amendment: while the poor villains (chief ministers of his wickedness, now betrayed by the author thereof) were delivered to many cruel sorts of death; he so handling it, that it rather seemed, he had rather come into the defense of an unremediable mischief already committed, than that they had done it at first by his consent.

If you want to pursue the question of Shakespeare's sources for *King Lear*, you will find them collected in Bullough *Narrative and Dramatic Sources of Shakespeare*, each* extract being prefaced by an editorial introduction discussing how Shakespeare used it in his own text. A briefer discussion of the issue will be found in Kenneth Muir's introduction to the Arden edition of *King Lear*, which is supplemented with shorter extracts from the sources in an appendix.

*Bullough, G. (ed.) (1973) *Narrative and Dramatic Sources of Shakespeare*, vol. 7, Routledge and Kegan Paul, pp. 269–420.
†Muir, K. (ed.) (1952) *King Lear*, The Arden Shakespeare, Methuen, pp. xxvi–xlii.